GUIDE TO SELF-PUBLISHING POETRY

FORMATTING, PRINTING AND MARKETING

By

ROY E. PETERSON

TRICROWN BOOKS

Guide to Self-Publishing Poetry
Formatting, Printing and Marketing

By Roy E. Peterson

**Cover Credit: Queen Marie Antoinette as Erato,
By Ludwig Guttenbrunn, 1788**

Published on behalf of TriCrown Books by Kindle Direct Publishing,
June 11, 2021.

ISBN-9798516118784

Questions: _Kindle Publishing_ or _tricrownbooks.com_
Available for sale on _amazon.com_ and _Kindle.com_

FOREWORD

There is no difference in the self-publishing needs of classical poets and modern free verse poets. Both will benefit from this Guide.

Self-publishing is one of the primary modern methods to make an initial impact on the consciousness of consumers and book publishers. From formatting and printing to marketing and sales, the landscape is littered with the hopes of writers who often must learn only by experience the best ways to present their literary legacies. To be sure, there are several self-publishing guides that generally cover the spectrum of all book genre, but I have learned over time there are special needs for poets to produce and disseminate their works.

This *Guide to Self-Publishing Poetry* is my endeavor to assist even the seasoned poet in the production and distribution of their cherished poetry. I have learned much over the course of five years of self-publishing. That qualifies me to offer at least observations and suggestions to improve the critical path to success. As for doing actual classical poetry writing, I recommend *How to Write Classical Poetry* by Evan Mantyk, et.al. He is the President of the Society of Classical Poets. There you will find the structures of the various classical forms, techniques, and meanings of the experts in writing classical poetry.

You will find that I prefer to write as I teach – in a folksy style that is me talking to you. Examples of my personal development in the continual desire to improve my poetic presentations serve to amplify the points I wish to make while doing so in a style that is neither stilted, nor ostentatious. My primary desire is to communicate with each of you with clarity and without ambiguous ramblings.

Poets who employ these tactical concepts will benefit greatly by reading this volume and are encouraged to purchase it for their own benefit.

Roy E. Peterson
San Angelo, Texas
June 10, 2021

TABLE OF CONTENTS

ENGRAVING

The Distrest Poet, John Hogarth, 1740.

CHAPTER 1

FORMATTING

The *Society of Classical Poets* website contains some wonderful educational tools for those of us who began writing poetry out of love for the genre, but who were not educated in the details of how to do it correctly. For those of us who thought *dactyl* might have something to do with a duck's webbed foot, we read and learned it is a meter in poetry that has one accented syllable followed by two unaccented ones, or one long and two short ones. Whether writing a Shakespearean Sonnet in proper iambic pentameter, or writing poems in various meters, I recommend going to the website and studying how poetry is approached by classical professionals. I include persistent, inveterate, acclaimed amateurs in the concept of professional, whether earning money, or not from their poems.

This Guide is meant to take poetry and other books once completed through the rest of the process to self-publication. It is not intended to cover the mechanics of the classical or modern free verse poetry writing process itself. Getting a poem to an audience in the best and most cost effective way in this digital age is something I learned in recent years that I will share with you. I refrain from making a recommendation as to which blogging, web builder, web host, or printer to use. I refuse to try them all for a temporary period of time to find out how those services work and why they fit my own set of preferences. You might say I just fell into mine. One came from researching how to save costs. The other came when the company I was using for templates and printing was absorbed by another company.

Self-publishing usually is the only way to begin to make an impact on the profession. According to BookBaby, "No other genre of **book** is as associated with **self-publishing** as the **poetry book**, or **chapbook**. Whitman, Eliot, Poe, Pope, Shelley, Cummings, Browning, and so many other **poetry** greats all paid to publish their first **books**." (Source: BookBaby, bookbaby.com/poetry-book-printing.)

When starting to write poetry seriously, I still had several questions and conceptions that pervaded my mind in my intellectual progression to become a poet with a modicum of acceptance within the Society and the community of classical poets. I hasten to add there are no admonishments, or rules locked in stone; just my observations for consideration. I also wish to make the point here and in other places in the Guide that this book is intended for all poets who decide they want to self-publish a book of poetry.

First, the basics of producing a readable eye-pleasing manuscript. There are two time-savers for any writer: the layout of the manuscript and outlining. Think of the layout as the foundation that establishes the underpinnings for everything else. Then think of outlining as establishing the basis for the entire book organization plan of action. The two foundations are indispensable to the superstructure of each production.

Consistency is the key characteristic that enhances the reader's experience. I know. You thought it was the blazing glory of each poem. I do not seek to denigrate anyone's poetry, but our goal here is to maximize reader contentment with the content. Anything out of the ordinary can distract the reader for the rest of the book. When might the reader encounter that anomaly again? The mind worries and wonders.

LAYOUT

One thing about layouts: everybody has one. A wide range of preferences come into play when we decide to layout the manuscript. Choices abound beginning with paper size that sets the height and width of the book. There are industry standards and then there are personal preferences. I erred in my layout on the side of industry standards, since that permits the book to fit into convenient and what has become traditional niches. The book fits on the shelf of the reader and that is exactly what we want it to do. We can forget about orientation, since virtually all poetry fits into portrait format.

Tip: Depending on who prints your book, you may need to reach 140 pages or more to have the title and your name placed on the spine of the book for ease of future reference.

Discussion of the major layout variations is as follows:

1. Book Page/Paper Size: Every book I have in every genre self-published in the last few years is in a 6"x9" book page size, except one. That was decided back when I had a publisher/printer that told me 8.5x8.5 inches was ideal for presentation of the story related to my cat, Albert, for juvenile consumption.

There is always the 8.5"x11" for Letter size, 8.5"x14" for Legal size, and all sizes in between. I found 6"x9" is a preferred industry standard. For my poetry it makes the most sense. My printer/publisher company has that size for one of their primary templates.

2. Borders: Placement of classic borders on classical poetry sounds, well, shall I say it, classic. For me they are distracting. I only use one border at the bottom and that is preferred by my printer, probably because it means less ink than having one on the top, as well. I use the border and place the page number under it. That is merely a preference, as many classical poets do not use any border. I never would place a border for decoration, or any other purpose on the sides.

3. Chapters/Sections: Here is where I can give you a lot of personal advice. When I write a book of classic poetry, I always insert ten poems per chapter. Why ten? It just seems natural to me. My minimum number of poems after completing my first two books became 100 poems. Almost all my original works have 100 poems. My biggest compendium has 300.

In mentioning the classic fit of poetry and art, I alluded to the fact that every book, except my recent one has dividers of the chapters or sections. I vacillate between the terms for the two, since I stopped using the word chapters and just place a number for the section or divider at the top of the new page. This book is an exception, since it has no poetry.

OUTLINING

My high school English teacher, who was an excellent teacher, and my mother who taught English in high school agreed that an outline is the only way to begin a manuscript. I had no choice, but to outline, and I thank them for that wisdom.

The benefits of an outline are to organize thoughts in a pattern, intensify the focus on one thing at a time, and decide on whether to put the important material first, last, or in the middle for maximum effect. Furthermore, it allows for ease of rearranging the pieces of the manuscript puzzle.

Writing classical poetry is different for me from writing a book such as this one. For poetry I do not begin the outline until I have written 40 to 50 poems. That helps me determine the categories of the poems and make an educated placement to fit a then planned topical heading. Then I prepare the outline. The outline is in the form of a Table of Contents. After writing about half the poems I intend to place in my classical poetry volume, I have a good fix on the categories into which I will divided the book and then place the poems in that framework in alphabetical order within those divisions. If poems fall outside those categories I either save them for later, or I make the tenth section a catchall category without using the term "miscellaneous." I just don't like the term.

Each poem I write after that I make sure to type in the title in the table and then insert the poem alphabetically in the text of the format. Even with only half the projected number of poems inserted, I print out the Table of Contents and compare with those placed in each section. I find sometimes I misplaced a poem in the wrong category, or not placed it at all. After that first check, I usually do not make a mistake in placement. I just make sure then I type the title into the table, I also insert the poem.

Some of the topical headings rhyme. After so many books of classic poetry, I have begun to use a typical pattern for consistency of placement in all my books. I am going to give you my primary categories. You will see that my categories far exceed any one book, but they can serve as a guide for you in planning your own categories and Table of Contents.

Here is my typical list of categories and usual order of presentation in the Table of Contents:

- *Love*
- *Romance*
- *Humor*
- *Nostalgia*
- *Wit and Wisdom*
- *Advice*
- *Political*
- *Patriotic*
- *Christian*
- *Holidays*

These ten category often are exchanged for others based on the number of poems I have written on a subject, or that I may then plan to write to fill up the category. These alternate categories include, **Country, For the Kids, Inspirational, Morals, Mystical, Myths, Nature, Regional** (like **Texas and Texans**), **Satire, and Seasonal.** I save the few poems that fall into some other categories for a future book.

      4. Columns: I never saw a need for two columns in a classical poetry book. I would rather extend the poem to the next page.

      5. Margins: I use left justified alignment. That way everything lines up perfectly. Then you can maneuver at the end of lines anyway you would like. It maintains consistency at the start of every line. Then I can apply tabs as wanted and needed. The norm is 0.5 inches on the left hand margin and one inch above and below the text of a poem. For poetry, though, once the title had been centered, the text should be tabbed once or twice to fit, or if too long, then begin at the left margin.

6. Pagination: What could go wrong with pagination? For one thing the page numbers better match with the Table of Contents. I still do my Table of Contents manually, just to make certain I have every poem I intended to publish and that it matches the page on the table. More than one time I have had to make a post-production change, because after my umpteenth editing book review, I made a change to a page that shortened it or made it longer, thereby affecting the corresponding pages sometimes by as much as an entire half page. Adjusting the top and bottom margins is one of the last things I do.

Placement of the page number is certainly open to debate and taste. Some love it on the far right at the bottom, some on the far right at the top (traditional placement), some at the middle of the page top or bottom, and the rare bird that puts in to the far left, virtually hiding it after the book is bound. I always put my page numbers at the bottom middle, but that is my taste and preference.

COVER DESIGN

As poets, we like to believe we are functioning in a reader world where pure intellect, abstract conceptualization and logic reign supreme. That is far from the case. Books are a product of designers, whether by ourselves or someone hired. Visual design is imperative to enhance reader pleasure and experience, not to mention sales and marketing. I believe you can tell a book by the cover, certainly by the title and the cover art. Then there is the important Back Cover Blurb as I call it that is inserted on the surprise, back cover.

Book titles and cover art contribute to this visual representation of our poems. My favorite title of one of my books is, "As the World Burns," an allusion to the long-running television soap opera, "As the World Turns." The subtitle is "Poetry by the Fireside."

As to Cover Art for poetry, I prefer anything from the 1920's back to the distant past. For one thing, I do not have to pay for use of the art or illustrations. Anything after about 1923, likely is copyright covered and will require payment, which I can obtain for $50 to $150 for licensing permission. Sometimes I have obtained licensing permission with no remuneration required.

A second reason for using classic art is there is a great choice of possibilities for classical art to fit classical poetry depending on the subject and my tastes in art.

Tracking down usability is a major issue. When using *Bing* as my search engine and going to images, at least I can see an enhanced image. There is a button for "pages" that employ the same work of art in their website. I can traipse through Pinterest, World Press, Fine Art and a series of other sources to find the title, artist and date when the original art was done. Pinterest by the way always seems to have more art pinned to their site than any other place. They also show related pictures in the righthand column that can assist me should I see something preferable. The problem is posters do not take the time to find the pertinent details of who, what and when.

Allow me a brief diversion here to pontificate on the free use or licensing permission required to use a vintage work of art on the cover and as section or chapter dividers.

Complete Information Desired

I wish every image online was required to show all three elements (title, artist, date), but less than 20% do. That percentage is my estimate and it may be high. That means I lose considerable time in finding an appropriate image, ensuring it meets the criteria for free use, and then be able to identify everything about it that I want in my cover and sectional dividing art.

I have spent as many as three to five days tracking down the information desired for ten art inserts and learning if there was a fee or not. So many of the beautiful artworks are posted to Pinterest, but, as I already said, there is no requirement to have any of the three informational elements I regard as important.

Avoid Paying the Image Factories

Image factories like Getty, Alarmy, iStock, and Fine Art often require subscriptions or payment for use of art that they have curated and in some cases enhanced to make lighter or more colorful. Either pay or beware the use of their image and find the same piece of art in another source. I would love to have them barred for charging for images of art prior to 1923. There is no need to pay a subscription fee for art from over a century ago. If I cannot find the desired art without using their site, I simply find a replacement.

Best Chance to Find Free Vintage Art

I hate to pay for cover art, mainly because the books of poetry I have self-published have insufficient sales to even pay for the cover art. From my own experience, I found *Wikimedia Art* and *Wikimedia Commons* websites offer the best chances for finding classic art that may be freely used as long as there is some mention of a common license associated with the use, since someone took the picture of the art and wants some credit for it. This is often the only place to discover the title, artist and date of the painting.

Other options are wallpaper and clipart; however, be aware that wallpaper art, while free to use online, may be from a copyrighted source and require licensing permission for commercial use.

FONT SELECTION

Published poetry should employ a font with serifs. This point is made over and over in the literature about how to print a book. A serif is additional short strokes added to the long strokes of letters to make them more eye-pleasing. A paucity of serif swishes, though, is preferred compared to extensive swishes that slow down the reading of a printed passage.

A typesetter for a book, magazine, or advertising, looks for fonts that provide clarity for easy-to-the eye reading and text that is legible even when the font is in small print. Traditional fonts are used because the subconscious recognizes them instantly and they do not distract and detract from content. The baseline letters must look like they belong as placed and not seem to dance around. The serif fonts have a greater beauty about them and that is important for typesetting classical poetry.

A book cover may benefit from a departure from these rules, since beauty in the elegance of some fonts is perfect for a title. I favor Cinzel Decorative myself for the cover.

Having gone through a brief litany of characteristics for choosing the perfect font, what do the experts say? In my research I have found the Garamond font is the preferred one, especially for classic poetry. A *Huffington Post* article on fonts echoed what I found in various Internet forums. Garamond is the preferred typeface font. As the article articulated: "Garamond is so obviously the best font that it would be offensive to try to justify it. It's timeless, elegant, understated and has every detail just right. Long live Garamond, greatest of all the fonts." (Source: *A Totally Definitive Ranking of Fonts* by Claire Fallon, 7/28/2014, huffpost.com/entry/font-ranking.) The next four in the ranking were Baskerville, Helvetica, and Times New Roman. Nowhere on the list was my favorite, Book Antiqua.

I will show you the differences in sizing, compaction, and elegance by typing in the words Classical Poetry below to allow you to compare them according to your individual taste and sense about industry standards using the ones above.

Baskerville:	Classical Poetry
Book Antiqua:	Classical Poetry
Garamond:	Classical Poetry
Helvetica:	**Classical Poetry**
Times New Roman:	Classical Poetry

I immediately tossed out Helvetica, because of size of the footprint each letter leaves when I am fighting for size of the verses and keeping one line rhymes, not ones with a drop down of one or two words that looks awkward on a page. Besides the size, there is no serif unless you count the "y". That is critical, especially for classical poetry. Of course, the *Huffington Post* article was not specific to the presentation fonts for classical poetry, was intended for the publishing trade. I included it here to show the great difference better serif fonts make.

The four remaining fonts pass the serif test. Garamond has the advantage of being more compact and allowing a few more letters on a line which can be a word or two, thus making the difference of having the entire sentence or phrase on line without finding a way to make it look better like I sometimes do by dividing the line of poetry somewhere near the middle for all the lines to make the rhyme look better.

Tip: You must use a serif font. I know! I promised only suggestions and recommendations, but I cannot emphasize this enough. You do want our readers to have a great reading experience I presume.

You likely noted that this Guide is in a size 14 Font. A size 12 font is the usual standard for normal publication. A size 16 font is the usual minimum standard for readers with sight impairment.

I purposely used a size 14 Font for most of this book and for the verses of Poems. I do reduce the Font to size 12 for the material in the front to save some space and because it is not as important as the text. Size 12 improves the look of the Table of Contents and my list of authored books.

GRAMMAR AND PUNCTUATION

To say that punctuation is fluid in poetry is an understatement. Some punctuation is essential in my mind, if for no other reason than clarity of the poet's meaning and intentions. Sometimes a single comma makes a great difference. An example given by my high school English teacher is: 1.) What's on the road ahead? versus 2.) What's on the road, a head? Another good example without me having to slightly change the word is 1.) Let's eat, grandma, as opposed to 2.) Let's eat grandma. See the difference punctuation makes?

One of the distinctions between classical poets and modern free verse poets is the use of punctuation. Classical poets stick to grammar rules. The rest do not. Those that do not use perfect punctuation, however, have their reasons related to presentation of their free verse.

Commas and Clarity

One of the first rules of poetry is clarity. Your words can run on forever in your mind, but to communicate with another human being requires some punctuation, if only to end a sentence and a thought. Beyond this first punctuation rule of clarity, poets may purposely and successfully ignore the rules to regulate thoughts, induce speed patterns and include pauses for dramatic effect. Commas affect thought processes and idea collections as do capital letters, semi-colons, dashes, line breaks and verses.

Modern American English has dropped the second comma in a series of three and before the "and" in even longer lists. Commas are still important.

Are you paying attention, e.e. cummings! My mother who was an English and Latin high school teacher would not have let you graduate.

Capitalization

I have favored capitalization of nouns, since I became fluent in German in the military. I also was fluent in Russian and Vietnamese, but I liked German capitalization. I will often capitalize an important noun in the middle of a line of poetry to emphasize a point I am making, to show reverence for someone or something, and to draw attention of the reader to the word while savoring the noun. You will find several examples of how I use it in this book.

Poet Debate over First Word Capitalization

The debate of capitalizing the first word of each line of a poem is another matter. All the "old time" poets thought it was a necessity including William Shakespeare. Read his works and all lines begin with a capital letter, even if it is not the beginning of a new sentence. I share an affinity for capitalizing the first word of each line regardless, but that does not mean a modern Classical Poet must do so.

One Space After Period

Those of us from an older generation were taught to add two spaces after a period before beginning the next sentence. Those rules changed with the modern print age to save newspaper space, or so some say. The eyes of readers have been conditioned now to view their reading material with one space.

Tips: Believe it or not, one tip I learned was to put it on my editing checklist, oh yes, I said checklist to ensure your poems and frontispiece materials all contain one space and not two from a period. The second tip is that in my word processor application, I can use the "Find" function from the upper right corner, open the program and make a universal change by typing in the "Find and Replace" fields a period and two blank spaces for "Find," then in the "Replace" field a period and one space.

Indentation Standard

Editors of book mostly adopted .5 inches as the standard indentation for paragraphs. You may have a format template given you that does this, or you may have to set it buy going to "Paragraph" in the toolbar, look under "Indentation," then under Left" and type .5. Under Special choose "First line" from the drop down menu. Don't forget to click "Apply" if that is in your program. You may do it for this one document, or make it a default program by going to the bottom of the menu.

Paragraphing Conventions

More choices for you here. Now that you set the indentation distance, you may either write paragraphs justified fully to the left and then make one space between them, or indent. I just know you are curious as to the reason why I chose to add a space in this text, rather than indenting, except for doing both with the numbered subheadings. I could answer like someone in you past used to do, "Because I can." That would not be satisfying. You will note that in this Guide I use a rather unusual indenting method, but it certainly is not a foreign way of indenting. Rather than indenting every paragraph, I chose to indent only those with numbers. The rest of the paragraphs are not indented; however, I do add a space between paragraphs. My reasoning is this method better sets off the points I am making paragraph by paragraph. It may be unorthodox to the traditional writer, but certainly is part of mainstream writing. Besides, book publishers will tell you they prefer the first paragraph of a chapter not be indented anyway. I believe you will quickly become used to my mixed method of indenting. It matters little to a poet as a writer, since the focus is on the poem verse indentation and not paragraph indentation.

I have so many individual subparagraphs with pertinent points, I decided it was better to separate the thoughts and discussions with the added space. What it does is give at least a millisecond pause for ingestion of the previous information and alerts the reader to the presence of a new thought.

In the Nonfiction book industry, furthermore, the first paragraph of any chapter is no longer indented. Neither are subheads or material following a numbered, or bulleted list. Fiction authors are adjured, on the other hand, to always use indented paragraphs without any page breaks. Remember we are dealing with a Nonfiction category, though, and may take liberties.

Your main goal of indenting is consistency. For poetry verses there are options. If you center the poem, both the start and end points of each line are uneven, but some find that attractive. For modern free verse poetry I have noted some unusual indenting, but that is allowed and indeed may enhance the points made or visualization of what the author wishes to communicate more real. I have seen everything from pyramids to pictorial representations.

That reminds me! I would like to lobby for poetry of any type to be pulled out of the Fiction and Nonfiction bifurcated categories and made a totally Independent genre. Most poets I know of any type mix the two categories in a book so it is neither fish nor fowl, but something else.

For the time being my publisher still has poetry listed under Nonfiction by their format, so I must remember to always check into that category for digital book sales purposes. Only in their book description and keywords can I present the separate categories into which it falls, like humor or romance. Besides, I cannot advance on their template without inserting the category.

ART AS SECTION DIVIDERS

Classical Poetry and Classical Art belong together. In a book of poetry, art is best used to divide the sections or organize thoughts like advice, history, humor, love, nostalgia, wit and wisdom. Even when keeping the costs down with black and white pictures, illustrations, or paintings, the experience of reading the poems in that section seem to have increased value and validity.

You will find that once printed, my art dividers are no longer in color. My printer charges a considerable fee for color printing of chapter/section dividers, so for the sake of providing a lower cost to the consumer, I opt not to pay for color production internal to my **softcover** book.

A **hardcover** book, however, may benefit from color plates included. My publisher recently provided a hardcopy option. I decided in a book I prepared of my very best poetry to opt for color dividers. The result is spectacular, but so is the cost. The royalty payment price went from around paying the printer about $20 per copy for a 400 page book to $62 per copy, prior to my royalty payments. I bought one and I would be amazed if I eventually sold ten copies. On the other hand, I plan to give them to my children and grandchildren for posterity, so I will buy more for myself.

CATALOGING AND DATES

I set down the date of every poem I have written. This is one of my methods of organization mentally, but it also gives me a context of the times that may be important at a later date. All poets should think in terms of future biographers and assisting them in their research. Think of it as an historical marker.

Cataloging poems alphabetically helps me find a poem for my own future publication, reference, or revision.

POET NOTES

I come from a graduate educational background that includes history, political science, and global business management. Footnotes or Endnotes were profusely sprinkled about if I had even an inkling someone had said something, or wrote something down in a passage that I quoted. Poets, I have found, are much less likely to cite a source, especially if that source is mentioned in the text of the poem. I do use Poet Notes at the end of a lot of my poems to provide information as to where the material was derived. I leave that to the discretion of the poet, but there are other notes that I tend to make on my poetry that may be useful for others to consider.

1. Comparisons: There may be passages alluding to previously written poetry, books, or articles that are important to understanding why you wrote what you did. For example, I titled one poem, "I Cannot Count the Ways I Love You." That was not a swipe at Elizabeth Barrett Browning's poem, "Let Me Count the Ways." Reading her poem in fact allows for continual counting, but these days, readers may or may not be acquainted with Elizabeth and her poetry. Besides, I thought my title more romantic. My other choice (in my mind) was to place the texts side-by-side, or over-under for comparison.

2. Credits: I still believe in noting from whence came my ideas on some poems, especially with a partial quote, or what I consider to be their original idea. Furthermore it is a way to give credit to a friend or enemy. The friend will be thrilled, since in a sense they feel immortalized by being in a book of poetry. The dividends are them telling others what you did for them. This is for kindness and good will, not for the thought of selling more books, although that may be a positive result.

3. Explanations: If I judge my thoughts in the poem to be too elliptical, as in an allusion, or allegory that I believe will elude the common reader's thoughts, I will provide a brief note to draw their attention to the need for their further reading of tangential material, or to read the poem again and attempt to envision what I had in mind.

4. Information: Poems often lack an essential item or two of information that can enhance the reader's experience.

Sometimes it is necessary to set a poem in context of time or place. As time telescopes on out after our demise, a poet note regarding the contextual time will help future generations understand it in terms of our environment. this supplements my dating of when I wrote a poem

5. Motivation: I rarely provide my motivation for writing a poem. That should be inherent in the poem itself, but once in a while it makes sense to me to write a brief note about why the poem was written in the first place. Think of it this way--it may be useful to your eventual biographers.

6. Multiple Meanings: I usually do not bother noting double meanings. That is the fun of poetry and usage of language that even the casual reader might understand. Triple meanings are trickier. Sometimes though, I have placed a disclaimer I thought was important, so as not to mislead the reader.

7. New Word: If I use a new word that does not appear in the dictionary, I want the reader to know they cannot find it, but it is a valid extrapolation from another word, and that the new word should be included in dictionaries in the future. The term for this manufacturing of a new word is *sniglet.*

LOGO

TriCrown Books made for the Author, Roy E. Peterson

22

CHAPTER 2

PRODUCTION AND QUALITY

Poets have a wide range of capabilities, perfectionism, audiences, and tolerances for editing their own work. I looked up the production of some of the great poets from the past and concluded their fame was founded upon a few poems that were deemed great and then became part of the history of great poetry. I found the following production of some great poets:

- **Dickinson:** Over 1,700. Only 12 published in her lifetime.
- **Frost:** 105-143 depending on what is counted.
- **Longfellow:** 153, but some of them are long.
- **Poe:** 50 (some variance here also).
- **Riley:** 1,000 approximately.
- **Scott:** 151.
- **Shakespeare:** 38 plays in verse, 154 Sonnets, 2 long narrative poems and scattered others.
- **Percy Bysshe Shelley:** 324.
- **Whittier:** 100 about.
- **Whitman:** 392.

The "Guinness Book of World Records" reports the most prolific English language poet was the Englishman, John Bradburne 1921-1979). Bradburne completed about 6,000 poems written mostly in a ten year period (1968-1979). His line count output of 169,925 (and still counting due to the fact many of them were in letters) almost doubles Shakespeare's output of 87,668 lines of poetry.

The point is the numbers of poems written is not essential to acclamation, but the audiences, the verbal gymnastics, the rhyme flow and other factors that were judged then and now as the greatest are what count the most. We may believe we have written the greatest poem ever written, but it is the public and critics that decide, not us. Furthermore, exposure of the poem (marketing, or any other means) is essential.

On a personal note, when I self-publish my next book of poetry, likely in July 2021, I will have published 4,000 original poems. Some of my volumes are compendiums by subject, such as love, sonnets, advice, patriotism, nostalgia, holidays and my best selected ones. I went through several chapters of my poems and average five verses and twenty total lines. Thus I estimate I have written 80,000 lines of poetry.

I have no compunction to challenge Bradburne for total poem count and line count. That means I am more concerned with quality. Right? Not exactly. Quality is subjective. I simply want my poems to be worth reading and become loved by others.

EDITING TIPS

1. Adjusting Poems: I always adjust every poem I wrote on the page for publication. The lateral adjustments are usually one or two tabs per line. On an MSWord program, I learned I can take the cursor, highlight the entire poem and then tab the entire poem to the right at one time without going line by line. For some reason, on occasion the poem disappears. You may already know how to prevent that, but as for me, when it happens, I just click the refresh arrow in the upper left and the poem reappears. It rarely happens now, because I learned another trick. First I always move the verses to the right one tab and then can move backwards as I please with the entire set of verses.

Adjustments of the verses on the page, so they do not split at the bottom and continue with half the verse on the next page, is solved by adjusting the height between each verse by clicking in the numbered window after the font face name and for example, reduce the size of the space from 14 to 10. Another trick I learned is that one can highlight the verses needing adjustment, right click, click on "Font" and change the size to an intermediate one, for example, "13". Usually I can only click above from "14" to "12" to "10" and so on. This is particularly valuable for longer lines in a verse that tend to have one or two words drop below the main line.

2. Beyond the Spellchecker: By all means run the spellchecker at the end, but consider that a rough review. Spellcheckers still cannot find missing words, homonyms, or misused words and they accept a word that is another word. I will give you an example. When I was editing this text, I found that the word "still" after "Spellcheckers" above was "till."

3. Checklist: Professional editors will tell you, trust me, that they do not make a one time run through the document and make all editing comments or changes based on that one editing run. Instead, editors go through with one category of factor focus at a time, such as 1.) Word usage, 2.) Punctuation, 3.) Margin adjustments, 4.) Numbering of section and chapters, 5. Capitalization, 6.) Picture sizing to make sure it fits inside the paper parameters, and 7.) Comparison of the Table of Contents pagination with the actual pages. By now my checklist is in my head and drives me to make successive edits.

4. Grammar Check: There are programs, of course, to check grammar, but they are not perfect either. If one is editing a product themselves and not paying an outside editor, they better be certain they know all the rules of grammar and have kept up to date with the changes, such as the one mentioned elsewhere in which there is now only one space after a period to the next sentence, rather than the two I learned when I was taking typing in the early 1960's.

5. Regional Accents: I have to laugh at accents, since they affect how poetry is read in everything from syllable counts to articulation of the spoken word. The best some can do is approximate traditional English pronunciations and hope the poetry flows sufficiently to be accepted. If one is writing with a purposeful regional accent, one must check for consistency of the accent and punctuation, such as replacing "ing" at the end of a word with "in'" to include the apostrophe.

I also learned that in common American English pronunciation, words like every are pronounced in two syllables and not three. This is an important point for classical poets, since meter is highly important. Before I learned this pronunciation was the acceptable one, sometimes I put an apostrophe in the word for the absence of the middle "e," as in ev'ry. I no longer have to do that. I read that the word "fire" is considered a one syllable word for pronunciation unless it is used with the word, "higher," at which point it becomes two syllables.

6. Revisions: Revisions are important and come from careful editing and sometimes just letting the poem sit for hours or days. I find a fresh perspective often comes to mind when I return to the poem even after a few minutes of doing something else. Even in print there is no reason not to make a revision when you believe it necessary to the future enjoyment of the words. My printer allows post-production changes and that is important. They do reset the date of publication.

Strengthening Words: Strengthening words is an important part of revision. Beginning with little words like "and," "it" and "thing" one can find a one syllable word that is more descriptive as an adjective, adverb, or noun and enhances the poem immensely. Never fear the semicolon or dashes as a way to improve the story.

DOUBLE CHECKING

Double checking is not enough. Retrace the entire list of editing tips and read the entire manuscript thoroughly from the title to the last endnote one final time. Even it you pay someone to edit, surprisingly you are the best final editor of the entire book. No one else knows what is in your mind and how you want to present the material.

PRE-PUBLICATION AND LOGO

I was shocked when I learned I had become a Publisher! I thought the Printer was the Publisher. Afterall, they produced the final product. I knew I was self-publishing the book, but with my new printer about three years ago, I was considered the publisher. I suddenly had to make some adjustments. I needed a name for my publishing company, for which I was now the prime owner and CEO. I needed a logo for inclusion at the bottom of the back cover of the book. Fortunately, I had both from my previous business endeavors as President of my own international trading company.

1. Logo: My logo is the dividing artwork to begin Chapter 2. I had it done professionally a long time ago, so the cost is likely irrelevant these days. One can make their own with any number of programs and aps, or just by drawing an illustration or taking a picture. One should register and/or trademark their company name and logo, so there is no infringement on the territory. Afterall, the one that takes either can sue you for sole use and you could have to pay both an attorney and the one bringing suit for infringement.

2. Publishing Company: My international trading company was TriCrown. It was easy to convert the name by adding "books" to make it TriCrown Books with a website of tricrownbooks.com. Bring your imagination to the table and develop a name not being used. My company is simply a DBA (Doing Business As). Check your local, state and federal requirements for registration of a DBA. More on this in the next chapter.

ENGRAVING

**Fifteenth Century Print Shop, by Basilius Valentinus,
"ostensibly a 15th-century alchemist, possibly Canon of the
Benedictine Priory of Saint Peter in Erfurt, Germany….."
(Source: Wikipedia)**

CHAPTER 3

PRINTING AND PUBLISHING

BEWARE PRINTERS THAT TAKE ADVANTAGE

I begin this section with a warning to beware those printers that overcharge for services and underperform on delivery. There are so many that can draw you into their clutches with slick ads in various media and make it seem as if they are the only ones who are worth your time, effort and hard earned money. Without mentioning any names, my first publisher took advantage of my interest with exorbitant fees for everything from setup to marketing. I averaged $1,000 per book before I took another look and found CreateSpace that would at least print my book on-demand for free. CreateSpace has been absorbed by Kindle and still prints my book with their templates for free.

PRINTER OR PUBLISHER

These terms are now mixed in the digital age. The difference depends on whether the company says they print-on-demand, but you are the publisher. Confusing? Yes. You will see in my presentation that I now more or less use the terms interchangeably. For example, in searching for companies that I know are only printers and wish to remain that way, I find their comparisons under "self-publishing" companies. There is no need to worry about the distinction, except that a company identifying as a printer allows, indeed makes you form your own company, so that you can claim to have a publisher. I already mentioned my own publishing company name as TriCrown Books. The real key is getting the book into print and distribution to the book market.

In my research I found if I typed into my search engine, "top rated self-publishing companies 2021," I could comparison shop between ten and twenty companies rated as "best" by someone, or some organization. I could also do cross-comparisons of advantages and disadvantages by checking the data with different advisers on the net. Since each company seems to be rated differently in different years, make sure you have the most current lists of top-rated companies. The hardcover and softcover printer/publishing companies may not produce e-books, for example.

eBooks

From experience, there is nothing like the thrill of holding your own printed copy of a book you designed and wrote. Consider it as a potential for immortality to have something in print. I disagree with some of the websites that believe more ebooks are sold than hard or softcover books. Maybe they are in certain genre, but not necessarily in classical poetry books. My print copies far outsell my eBooks. I would almost say don't bother with ebooks, but then there will be the exception.

With many companies, such as mine, you can have your cake and eat it too. With my company I can virtually publish both simultaneously by inputting a PDF manuscript into the hardcover and soft cover categories and then an MSWord file into the eBook category for which I had the downloaded template and produced the document in the first place. In my case, I write in an MSWord program, but to publish in hard and soft cover, I have to convert the file to PDF for uploading. I still have the program in MSWord and that is all that is needed to upload the manuscript.

There is no need to bother with companies that represent major business enterprises. As classical or modern free verse poets, we are individuals that can obtain excellent services by being who we are and save the tremendous costs of a business enterprise. The options and choices are a bit overwhelming. There are so many out there who want to work with us and will do so in a safe and honorable environment with assistance in such things as marketing added to the moderate pricing or free printing.

PRINTER/PUBLISHER SELECTION

Main considerations for self-publishing are ease of self-production and self-editing, free printing or up front cost, marketing reach and costs of marketing, distribution to national and international markets, editing resources available internal to the printer/publisher, and royalties.

One caveat: up front costs may be saved in the long run, since the one-time payment may reduce or eliminate the royalties collected by the company. There are also monthly subscription fees by some that eliminate the initial up front cost and royalty payments. Study all the plans carefully to select the one best fitting your desires and circumstances.

I made a composite list by checking various printer ratings pages on the Internet and using my own preferences for determining which of them to use. One must study the features of each to come to an informed decision in the selection process. This is where needs determine choices. I am now relatively independent and can make one choice, but some of you may need more intensive guidance to achieve the best results.

There are four types of self-publishing companies. I believe it is important to know and understand those differences.

1. Aggregator: An aggregator means book distributor first and foremost. You likely will pay for the other services from editing the book to publication with another firm or themselves. There can be flat fees for the editing and usually a percentage of royalties deducted by the company prior to you getting a royalty check.

2. Retailer: A retailer has an online store, a physical store, or both as outlets for sales of your book. You likely will need a platform to market and sell your book, although the book is "stocked" in their own system. Retailers, though, will offer access to their marketing platforms for a fee to work with them, or their associated companies that do the work. When you go with a retailer, your book is also captive in their own retail system. That can be good or bad depending on your perspective. For me it meant at least having the book for sale somewhere daily.

3. Educator: These companies are more interested in selling courses for a potential author to learn how to self-publish and then apply those skills with their associated subcompanies or contracted firms from which they can also get a fee for delivering your product to them for printing. This book is all you need to do the same thing.

4. Service: Author services are provided piecemeal and they usually farm out those processes to other vendors that provide editing, cover design, printing, and marketing.

Here is my winnowed list in alphabetical order of the top 12 printer/publishers in 2021:

> Apple Books (Retailer)
> Barnes & Noble/Nook Press (Retailer)
> BookBaby (Aggregator)
> Draft2Digital (Aggregator)
> IngramSpark
> Kindle Direct Publishing (KDP) (Retailer)
> Kobo (Retailer)
> Lulu (Aggregator)
> PublishDrive (Aggregator)
> Reedsy (Educator and Service Provider)
> SmashWords (Aggregator)
> StreetLib (Aggregator)

Some printer/publishers are retailers, meaning they place the book in their own retail system. Apple, Barnes & Noble, KDP and Kobo have their own retail markets. Aggregators provide the widest automatic distribution. Educators/Service Providers assist with courses on how to do things and succeed with the self-published book. The outsourcing of services by some companies is not as complex as one might think, since they generally employ a one-stop input capability and they do the rest of the work to get it to top individual providers.

ROYALTIES

We need to get royalty percentages anticipated in our minds to understand the self-publishing industry and what we are getting. I struggled with the term "royalties" ever since I decided to self-publish seven years ago. What does it really mean and how can money paid for self-publishing be royalties? Well, my struggle is over and I am struck by lightning. I woke up. (Today, June 10, 2021) I made a discovery that changed my outlook. I read an online missive titled, "Royalties: The Seduction of Self-Publishing," in *The Independent Publishing Magazine* from February 13, 2015 that told me "In the strictest sense, there really is not such a thing as royalties in self-publishing" Talk about a strike from out of the blue, but it finally filled in the information void that I had questioned from the start seven years ago.

In the traditional publishing world I was aware that the publisher paid royalties of an agreed percentage to the authors of some size with 15-20% going to the agent that landed the deal. With the thought that royalties are indeed a seductive term as mentioned in the article title, what gives?

In self-publishing you likely are both the author and publisher as you will find out in this Guide. The article starkly states in the self-publishing world, an actual "royalty *IS* 100% of whatever is paid to the author!" unless others are involved. That told me a new word should be coined, or the word "royalty" dropped and don't try to change it to "commission." As the article indicates, "some companies like to play a game of math with authors."

Many of the printing/sales/marketing companies make it sound like you are getting the lions share because they state 70% royalties, but that is to them and it is not really royalties but their share of the entire pie. You are receiving a cash payment of a percentage of sale (not profit). The model is really a pay per book for publishing model, not a traditional royalty structure. Do the math yourself. There are alternative models out there where you pay everything up front and in fact receive the cash amount of sale, but they are extremely costly up front. If you have low sales, you will never recover what you paid. As the article says, "Remember, you are footing all or most of the cost of publishing of your book…" By the way, you do get a lot more back on eBooks depending on the sales price that **you** set.

PRINTING/PUBLISHING COMPANIES

I am now going to provide you with brief looks into the twelve listed companies above. I recommend extensive reviews besides this one before a final decision, but this can serve as a starting place to prioritize your search. I need to add a disclaimer here. The prices throughout for printers, blogging firms and website hosts are current as of June 2021, but subject to change and discounts may be offered.

Apple Books (Retailer)

If you own a Mac computer, then Apple Books is the way to go. That is because in order to publish to the Apple Store, you have to be a Mac user. If you are in that category, it is free to publish your printed book and to put it in their eBook system. The royalty rate for you is a flat 70% for most books sold.

Uploading a manuscript to the Apple system for publication is free and easy. Apple Books is the second largest online retailer of eBooks and you may upload to that portion of their system.

You must have a Mac computer, or else work through one of the aggregators such as those I listed. Unlike Kindle, there is no capability to read a book through the browser. You must enter their system which is in the ePub format and is not compatible with other platforms.

Barnes & Noble/Nook Press (Retailer)

Barnes & Noble Press is easily recognizable from their brick and mortar stores, but as those slow fade away, they have entered the digital age and kept a strong image and sales platform, especially for the eBook market. Through their Nook Press, a self-publisher can publish and sell directly to Barnes & Noble readers.

Uploads to their printing platform are free, easy and seamless. They have affiliations with some of the strongest service providers for production processes as needed such as Reedsy for editorial support, 99 designs for cover design and Inkubate for marketing. Less that 1% of books published make the shelves of their physical stores, but they are available online. They pay royalties in a range of 40-65% depending on the services needed and desired.

BookBaby (Aggregator)

BookBaby advertises as the easiest self-publishing/printer platform with which to work. The site offers a wide range of packages at a price with all the help a writer could want and who want to cover all self-publishing bases. The package that is lowest priced at $99 for publication has no frills meaning that the classical poet must learn everything from designing the cover to navigating the input template. That makes the package somewhat akin to Apple and KDP. Their comprehensive package is $1,990. See the chart of additional full service providers on page 42.

Book Baby does not dip into your royalties to take a commission on your sales. Everything is regarded as being paid up front, thus no commissions required.

Draft2Digital (Aggregator)

Draft2Digital (D2D) is a relative newcomer to the self-publishing industry but they have an aggressive help and assist program. Many of the SmashWords customers have migrated to D2D.

They have ease of upload and it is free with free formatting. They take only 10% of royalties and distribute to Amazon, unlike one of their main competitors. They provide access to international book links.

IngramSpark

Until Amazon absorbed CreateSpace, IngramSpark was the main storefront for authors. They are in a close relationship with KDP (think Amazon) to print and distribute hard copies via print on demand in national and international markets. There are upfront costs that are not charged by KDP; however, IngramSpark offers better quality and superior book bindings.

IngramSpark provides the widest distribution network to top online retailers, libraries, bookstores, schools and universities. KDP expanded distribution in fact goes through IngramSpark.

Kindle Direct Publishing (KDP) (Retailer)

If you remember, Amazon was incorporated in the first place to shake up and overtake the book industry by committing to online sales. Kindle Direct Publishing (KDP) is the self-publishing platform Amazon developed for authors to publish and print their softcover books and eBooks.

In 2021, KDP added two programs, a hard cover program and a chapbook size print publication that can easily be expanded over time by additional input to build a book or provide continual updates of new material.

KDP with the marketing power of Amazon is dominate in the industry. Amazon controls 40% of the self-published digital book publishing space. Their extensive reach is an important, since an author's book is available daily to millions of browsers daily.

KDP has competitive royalty rates of 35% for books priced under $2.99, or 70% for all books priced over that amount.

Variances are found in their international markets, which are also substantial, but the author/publisher is provided the information as to the percentages and sales prices in those markets prior to publication/printing. You are the publisher.

KDP offers a "Select Exclusivity" program for 90 days that includes perks such as special promotion programs. During that time your book is locked down exclusively to Amazon and it is not available on other platforms.

Kobo (Retailer)

Let me begin by disclosing that Kobo is part of the Japanese firm Rakuten and is based in Canada. Rakuten is the world's 14th largest online company giving their subsidiary Kobo a worldwide reach, especially for eBooks. An estimated 35% of all eBook sales in Canada are by Kobo.

Uploading manuscripts is described as free and easy on their self-publishing platform, Kobo Writing Life (KWL). Their competitive royalty structure is somewhat like KDP's with 45% if the book is under $2.99 and 70% over that book price. Kobo operates in 16 countries outside the US. They have over five million titles available in 77 languages. Like KDP, KWL provides a detailed sales analytic tool for authors to track daily sales.

Lulu (Aggregator)

According to online sources, Lulu is one of the oldest publishing platforms when they began publishing and distributing eBooks in 2009 and in five years became a publishing giant.

Uploading is regarded as free and easy. You must purchase your own ISBN, but when that is done the book is provided to all the major distribution and online retail outlets.

I learned that recently Lulu print books are farmed out to an Australian firm for $1,400.

In exchange, the author receive 80% royalties for print books and 90% for Ebooks sold.

Lulu sells author service including editing, cover design, formatting, promotion, and marketing. They do have their own bookstore to sell and distribute books.

PublishDrive (Aggregator)

PublishDrive is a relative newcomer to the self-publishing game, but already has become a major aggregator. PublishDrive is Apple approved and a Google partner, thus tapping into their vast resources for global distribution.

PublishDrive has a different payment model that most. They charge the author a monthly subscription rate and the author keeps 100% of sales royalties. Without the subscription the flat rate is still an impressive 10% only on sales. Their profits are more built into their subscriptions and up front costs for all the features needed to have a successful book on the market.

Reedsy (Education and Services)

Reedsy falls in the separate category of educator and servicer. In a sense the author has access to a wide range of resources and does not feel isolated by inputting to various platforms for their requirements.

Reedsy employs an outsourcing platform with considerable power connecting authors with editors, proofers, formatters, cover designers, marketing strategists and even ghostwriters. This sounds confusing, but Reedsy is a one-stop company, so the author inputs to one place and the bases are covered.

Do you want a query letter to traditional publishing companies? Reedsy will do it. Do you need an editorial assessment? Reedsy will do it.

SmashWords (Aggregator)

SmashWords predated its new primary competitors, Draft2Digital and PublishDrive that have begun to cut into their market with platforms that are easier to navigate and have more powerful setup tools.

Monthly payments are made for sales and distribution support, but the book is also listed on their own store platform. Authors earn up to 80% royalties if their book is so listed with the store.

You will be surprised, but SmashWords is the largest eBook distributor for self-published authors by working with the major retailers and outlets of Apple, Barnes & Noble and Kobo. The downside is they do not distribute to Amazon. Furthermore formatting is complex and time consuming. They do have a web design, but it was called "archaic."

StreetLib (Aggregator)

If your primary market is European, such my classical poet friends from the United Kingdom, then StreetLib may be an excellent choice. StreetLib is Italian-based. They also have a strong presence in Latin American. Their primary focus is international markets that include dashboards configured for several languages from English and Italian, to Hindi. They also have moved into the African book market.

StreetLib takes 10% of each eBook sale. There are the typical up front costs associated with all the services needed by an author.

KDP does provide a formatted template for both text and cover, book size choices, an ISBN and fill-in the blank capability on two pages to prepare the book for printing. One uploads the document in pdf format for softcover and various other document formats for the ebooks. One must learn how to do everything themselves, but there are guides to assist the beginner. They do have a limited choice of how the cover looks and limited color palette. You also must apply for the copyright yourself to the federal government, but with KDP you have the option of a free **ISBN**.

Tip: Why is an **ISBN** important? Every book that is published can (Must!) be given an International Standard Book Number (ISBN) which is used worldwide as a numeric identifier unique to each book. This 13-digit identifier is an absolute must if you plan to sell your book (bookstore or online retailer), or have it placed in libraries. If you are only publishing a book as a handout to friends and relatives, a local cookbook for a club, or for other noncommercial purposes, then and only then would you not need an ISBN.

Tip: Never pay for editing! (From "writersweekly.com" May 4, 2021)

For those requiring more support including marketing support, distribution, cover formatting and preparation and other tools. I am going to give you a comparison chart of associated costs for similar publishing/print packages to give you an idea of what you might expect to pay.

I learned I can do everything myself, except the marketing and believe classical poets are capable of the same, however, here is a comparison cost chart taken from "2021 Self-Publishing Price Comparison," *WritersWeekly*, March 4, 2021.

2021 Self-Publishing Price Comparison

BookLocker: $875
Balboa Press: $1,299
Westbow Press: $1,299
Trafford: $1,948
Bookbaby: $1,990
AuthorHouse: $2,053
Xlibris: $2,097
iUniverse: $2,118
Archway Publishing: $2,199
Breezeway Books (previously Llumina Press): $2,598
Fast Pencil / Opyrus / Infinity Publishing: $2,595
Xulon Press: $3,545
Mill City Press: $3,690
Outskirts Press: $3,795
Wheatmark: $6,000

This self-publishing comparison is for those who need full service assistance including marketing and distribution at the end of the process. This cost comparison excludes any editing fees.

PROOF COPY

You may feel your final proofing a copy now in print may be good enough for review on your computer screen. I assure you it is not. Better to delay the book and have a proof copy sent to you for final editorial review. That will delay final printing and the date the book is live for sale by a few days, but it is worth the time and effort. Things look different on the printed page. I am telling you this from experience. Another week should not matter,

VOLUME OR CHAPBOOK

I have always eschewed Chapbooks. I never liked the name, Chapbook. Believe it or not that is the reason for my prejudice toward them.

If a poet can write 40 to 60 poems, which is the normal chapbook size, then they can certainly write 100, unless they are completely focused on one subject area. This is a personal choice, but I prefer to publish a volume of poetry only after producing a minimum of 100 poems I believe worthy for the public to view.

Chapbooks in the industry, though, are often worth producing for limited venues such as local friends, local or regional organizations, for placing in airports, or restaurants, and special occasions. Chapbooks occupy a niche in readership focused on a specific theme and offer poetry in a small dose, usually around forty poems at most. Many classical poets use chapbooks for their first outputs to develop their craft and grow their readership.

PHOTO: AUTHOR'S OFFICE 2010

CHAPTER 4

WRITING AND WRITING PHILOSOPHY

WHERE TO WRITE

Finding a place to write is a matter of taste and individual capability to focus on the task at hand. Tom Clancy, the great Cold War spy thriller novelist wrote his first manuscripts after supper by typing at the kitchen table. How he succeeded is beyond me.

I need a place away from family and other distractions, although I do have a television or radio often playing in the other room to simulate company at home. I tune it out when I focus, but I am sure that is not the ideal writing environment. The pros will tell you seclusion from any noise is the obvious way to write, but I do not require absolute quiet to concentrate. Everyone to his own taste said the man who kissed the cow.

WRITING

All poets have their moments of inspiration, or else why would they write? My external stimuli come from a wide range of sources: my past experiences, something said by a friend or enemy, a book I read, a thought that comes to mind that gives me delight, a news article, a meme posted on social media and the entire ambient environment.

When writing, sometimes the inspired verse is the introduction and sometimes it is the perfect conclusion to my mind. I was taught to always have an introduction and a conclusion. Sometimes the conclusion comes to me in the middle of writing verses and I move it to the end and write toward that conclusion.

WRITING PHILOSOPHY

My philosophy on writing poetry is my own outlook and elucidation. Each of you will have your own modifications of writing and marketing mechanics.

Great artists like great poets do not necessarily aspire to greatness, but rather to elucidation of that which fascinates them to their own satisfaction. To be sure they are on a great quest to unlock secrets, detail events, resolve inconsistencies, further knowledge, and explore the eternal, whether that be in this world or the next. They wish to share their insights, visions, and beauty with everyone through their chosen medium of expression.

What makes paintings great, humor funny and contagious, and poetry meaningful? They all appeal to the senses of the common man, or woman; are enjoyed, because they engage the mind with their creativity; and thrill with how they elicit a viscerally exciting response within the heart. Cumbersome constructs that obfuscate these reactive pleasures of the senses, mind and heart with vagueness in a picture, or portrait; comical thoughts that are humorous only to a few; and indecipherable use of language in a poem may be judged great by the social snobs, those aspiring to demonstrate their erudition, and those who consider themselves superior in their interpretation of art for the masses, but fail to inspire the rest of the world seeking beautiful simplicity.

I admire classic art with definite form and detail, whether landscapes or portraits. From Michelangelo to Matisse, there are centuries of exquisite paintings that speak to the senses of the mind and heart. There is beauty in the naïve paintings of a Grandma Moses who conveyed simple concepts in regal beauty. Van Gogh is on the edge of my tastes, but acceptable for portraying colorful conceptualized reality. The Impressionist School of Painters with Claude Monet and Pierre August Renoir in the 1800's mated beauty of color and form with still discernible images. Howard David Johnson is a recent active artist whom I consider great for his vivid portrayal of historical and mythological figures using beautiful models and placing them in the historical or mythological context. The Artist of Light, Thomas Kinkade, who recently left this world, touches my senses with his landscapes incorporating homes, churches, and other meaningful substantive objects, because I can relate to his realistically fanciful paintings with my senses and my feelings.

I, for one, have never been inspired by modern art with its amorphous forms. I would never hang a chaotic Picasso on any wall in my home, nor most of the junk foisted upon us in the twentieth and twenty first centuries. I still laugh at an episode of *Colombo*, in which he finds himself in a modern art gallery befuddled by the paintings and sculptures with the exorbitant prices that have no meaning other than the title of the artwork. Looking at one black onyx-like sculpture with three bulbous appendages, he is informed that the title is "Spirit of a Dead Dog." His incredulous look matches mine at the nonsense of the piece and the audacious effort to sell it for several hundred dollars. Next he looks at a picture and has no clue what it is until the gallery guide provides the meaning that exists only in the title. Then he looks to the wall and asks, "What is the price of that?" The gallery guide looks aghast, because he is pointing to the covering for a ventilator.

The timeless humor of Mark Twain while hearkening back to another era, triggers a feeling of common cause and common virtue central to the morality and culture of every era. The simple similitudes and comparisons that elicited laughter by the humorist Will Rogers endure over the decades. Even Benjamin Franklin's tongue in cheek writings echo through the centuries.

Turning to poetry, I enjoy the simple humor of an Ogden Nash or a Doctor Seuss; thrill to the dark and mournful tones of an Edgar Alan Poe; love the clear descriptions of a Henry Wadsworth Longfellow; and relax with the poems of a Robert Frost rhapsodizing and detailing simple life and simple values using unpretentious country common terms and themes.

It would be dishonest and self deprecating to say that as a poet I do not aspire to greatness, but if I lost my sense of proportion, of individuality, of the common touch, then I would be but a tinkling cymbal, a shadow of myself, and a charlatan. Whether out of vanity, or foolishness, I would rather be discovered than to market my own poetry. On the other hand I believe that my poetry is educational, humorous, historically accurate, mythologically sensitive, romantic, inveighs against social and cultural degradation, and smashes untenable political concepts and icons.

Although I could write doggerel at the bottom of the scale, modern monologue poetry without rhyme, or poetry of the highest linguistic order, I choose to write for all levels of taste, from the blue collar worker and family to the highest levels of society and academia. Afterall, I thrived at all levels.

I purposely write so that every reader can understand my thought process, my realities, my fantasies, and my humor simply and comfortably reading or listening for themselves and feeling the heartfelt words which I hope to imbue with passion and perspective. Ultimately every reader is the judge of the value of the poetry and the poet. Each will find their own comfort level, comprehension of the poet's intent in writing the poem, and depth of feeling that the poems engender. Thus I leave it in your hands, mind, and heart.

ILLUSTRATION

Leary's bookstore stocked used and antiquarian books.
illustration on rear pastedown of blank book
Issued by the firm ca. 1880.

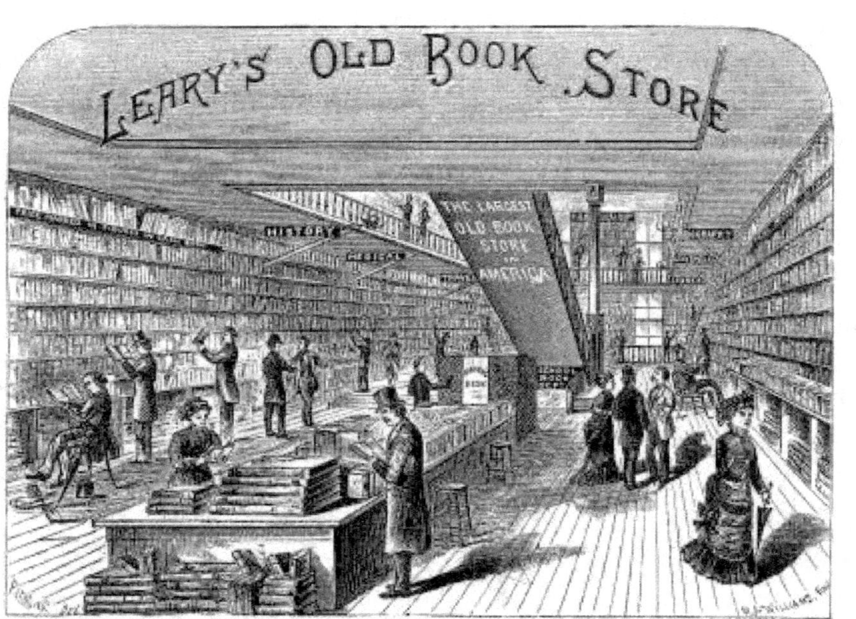

EDWIN S. STUART, No. 9 South 9th St., Phila.

CHAPTER 5

GUERRILLA MARKETING AND SALES:
LOCAL OUTLETS

You will note at this stage of my poetry writing, I have not exhibited a primary interest in marketing. Let me assure you, I have the capability, since I taught marketing at the university level. I have concentrated on writing poetry. When I focus, I zero in on the object of my primary interest at the time and concentrate on it until I have succeeded. My primary interest is still in writing. If I had the financial resources, I would find someone who would market my poetry for me. I do not have that luxury, so sometime soon I plan to focus on marketing. I have some preliminary notions of how to do it will be of interest.

Chapter 5 is my presentation of some of the guerrilla marketing methods that are proven to work. Chapter 6 is contests that provide an opportunity both to earn money and be recognized nationally or regionally for your efforts. For our purposes I will exclude blogging and websites from this chapter, but give them independent treatment in Chapters 7 and 8, respectively. Blogging and Websites are your marketing entry points for national and worldwide marketing efforts.

There are guerrilla methods of marketing like submitting poetry to a variety of periodicals like Readers Digest; having poems published in a broad range of poetry publications with regional, state, or national audiences; entering contests and hopefully winning; and encouraging my friends on social media to share my poems with others to elicit interest in my books. Targeting the right audience with the right poem is the essence of marketing.

The most effective method, however, is called Local Marketing. More poetry books are sold locally than by any other marketing method. You should particularly put them on your social media platform as reminders they make excellent gifts on occasions like Christmas and birthdays.

In a sense local marketing is a guerrilla method, but on an even lower scale—the grass roots level. Local outlets include taking an author copy of your book to a bookstore and giving a copy to the owner/manager for consideration of placing your book on the sales shelf; asking a bookstore owner to have a signing day for your books; local or nearby city events that allow vendor tables; and local literary guild or garden clubs at which you offer to speak or read some poetry appropriate to their venue.

BOOKSTORE STOCKING

Bookstore owner appreciate becoming acquainted with local writers and their books. They know that local authors tend to sell at least a few books from their shelves. My tactic is to take one of my author copies to the owner and give it to him or her free to read and keep. That greatly increases the chances they will stock the book on their shelves and maybe even place several copies in a prominent place in their store.

If you have any marketing tools to go with it, you enhance sales. It could be as little as bookmarks with a picture of the book on it, or it could be a standup board with advertising wording on it and a picture of you the author or your book. These can be manufactured relatively inexpensively.

BOOKSTORE SIGNINGS

Once you are assured the bookstore owner approves your book and will stock it, they like to have local authors in to sign books for a day or two. Why not, after all the space is available and they are not paying you directly to sit there and sign autographs.

CHAMBER OF COMMERCE

Chambers of Commerce are always looking for speakers. One can join the Chamber and attend their meetings for greater visibility. Some of them will let you place a copy with the chamber for perusal by visitors and smaller ones may even allow sales for a percentage of the take.

CLUBS

Garden clubs, book clubs, literary clubs and any other clubs that can relate to you book make excellent places to attend and speak. If one wishes, they can join or at least attend Lions Clubs, Rotary Clubs, the VFW, the American Legion and a host of others. Who knows, they might ask you to compose a dirge for a funeral ceremony.

Think outside the box. Why not attend the PTA, standup and announce you are contributing a book you just published to the library for the children to read.

CONVENTIONS

Even smaller towns and cities may have conventions. Many of them you do not know about unless you consult with the Chamber of Commerce. Once you find out they are scheduled locally, one can contact the organizers and either speak, or be allowed to set up a vendor table.

GIFTS

Giving a book as a gift to friends, relatives, and potential targets of interest may assist sales in the long run by word of mouth or placement in the home for visitors to peruse.

FLEA MARKETS

Flea markets may or may not be your "thing," but at least you can obtain a vendor table and likely cover the cost of the table with sales. The real advantage though is meeting people and telling them about your book and what a great gift it would make.

INTERVIEWS

One can arrange interviews with local journalists, radio announcers and television studios. They are all scrambling for news and here you are ready, willing and able as a filler interview for their paper or program.

LIBRARIES

Giving a volume to a city, high school, or university is an excellent way to impact local scholars or library visitors.

REUNIONS

Class reunions are an excellent source of sales, especially if there is some subject matter in the list of poems that nostalgically relates to the class, or that discusses historical events of the surrounding area, eulogizes some citizens from the hometown, and relates to the local physical environment.

My high school reunions are in three categories: 1.) All School Reunion every five years. 2.) All classes from the 1960's called the FAB 60's Reunion that meets annually. 3.) Class of XX Reunion that also meets annually.

The All School Reunion Committee allowed me to set up a table in the library with my books for sale. Why the library? Everyone seemed to pass through the library as part of their tour. Having a book for sale in the library as a memento of the Reunion made it a keepsake. I was asked to sign the books and make nostalgic references. It helped that some of the poems were nostalgic takes on events and incidents from the local area. I was also the speaker at the Reunion in 2015, so I achieved high visibility and acknowledgement.

The FAB 60's sets up tables on which I can place my books for sale along with tables selling green chili, homemade jams and jellies, and pickled jalapeño peppers. I also gave a free copy as a door prize and then got to explain what it was about in case someone had missed it at the table before the ticket was drawn for the winner. I later overheard the winner discussing my book at other tables with my friends.

My class reunion annually is a good place to take any books self-published since the last reunion. There I can talk personally about what I am doing and writing,

SPEAKING ENGAGEMENTS

Speaking opportunities come in many colors. One can join a Toastmasters Club, for example and become a speaker. One

can read an Independence Day poem at a city July 4th
celebration. I already mentioned the Chamber of Commerce
and Reunions as venues for speaking.

TRADE SHOWS

Trade Show organizers conduct trade shows to make money
for their organizations. Any vendor is welcome at these trade
shows, even though your product does not match any of the
fields of interest of their show covered by the term "trade."

DRAWING: SPARRING MATCH BY GRANGER
1800'S

CHAPTER 6

POETRY CONTESTS

Contests offer one of the best ways to earn money for poets. One of the best sources for monthly contests is provided by Adam Cohen in "Winning Writers." This can be accessed using the following url: Winning Writers, <adam@winningwriters. Another excellent source is provided by Hope Clark: <hope@fundsforwriters.com. There are others, but these are the two upon whom I rely.

The *Society of Classical Poets* has an annual poetry contest for classical poems of rhyme and meter with submissions near the end of each year and a first prize of $1,000 and cash prizes for additional placement. Also announced through the *Society of Classical Poets* is an annual Falun Gong classical poetry contest that takes place in the spring of each year on behalf of that organization with cash prizes.

Ardor Online Literary Magazine has a chart of "74 Poetry Contests that Pay," (Source: *Ardor Online Literary Magazine*: ardorlitmag.com. Cash award payments for first prize are listed along with the links for entering the contest. Fees are usually required. There may cash awards for second and third places and more, although they are not listed.

Classical poets need to check each contest for restrictive criteria such as who can submit (like racial groups, state residents, and other specialized groupings) then look at their past award recipients to see if any of them have been classical poets, or if there is a strong prejudice toward modern free verse poetry only having won in recent years.

There are contests that require a certain format, such as haiku or sonnets. Your submission will have to conform to the guidelines for writing such poems. Again I refer you back to the Society of Classical Poets and their book, "How to Write Classical Poetry."

Modern free verse poets simply need to reverse the process of discovery. Is the contest only for poems with rhyme and meter?

When reviewing poetry contests, one must determine whether a previously self-published poem can be submitted. This often is not easy to determine from the guidelines for the contest. Some contest guidelines simply state "previously published poems are not accepted," but they may make exceptions if the poem is self-published. They do not specify adequately, at least I have discovered that from my own experience.

Always review the poetry winners over the last three to five years to determine the type of poems that won by subject matter; length of poem; whether it was satirical, humorous, or serious; and use of words such as alliteration.

A final point to check on is the judges. Assess who they are and their biases by either reading their own poetry, or by seeing which contests they judged and comparing the outcomes of those contests.

POETRY CONTEST THAT PAY

My source for the contest list is "74 Poetry Contests that Pay: 2021 Contest Deadlines," – ARDOR, ARDOR Literary Magazine (ardorlitmage.com) ARDOR gave permission for anyone to use the schedule and give it to others to promote themselves and Contests.

January Poetry Contests

Mississippi Review Poetry Contest
Entry Deadline: 1/1/2021
Entry Fee: $15
Prize: $1,000

Bayou Magazine's Kay Murphy Prize for Poetry
Entry Deadline: 1/1/2021
Entry Fee: $20
Prize: $1,000

Gemini Magazine Poetry Open
Entry Deadline: 1/3/2021
Entry Fee: $5
Prize: $1,000

The Colorado Review Prize for Poetry
Entry Deadline: 1/14/2021
Entry Fee: $28
Prize: $2,000

The William Matthews Poetry Prize
Entry Deadline: 1/15/2021
Entry Fee: $20
Prize: $1,000

The Third Coast 2021 Poetry Contest
Entry Deadline: 1/15/2021
Entry Fee: $16
Prize: $1,000

Meridian Editors' Prize for Poetry
Entry Deadline: 1/25/2021
Entry Fee: $8.50
Prize: $1,000

Crazyhorse Prize in Poetry

Entry Deadline: 1/31/2021
Entry Fee: $20
Prize: $2,000

February Poetry Contests

Wisehouse International Poetry Award

Entry Deadline: 2/29/2021
Entry Fee: $5
Prize: $1,000

April Poetry Contests

The Magpie Award for Poetry

Entry Deadline: 4/17/2021
Entry Fee: $25
Prize: $500

USA Gold Pencils Student Poetry Contest

Entry Deadline: 4/29/2021
Entry Fee: None
Prize: $500

The Marsh Hawk Press Poetry Prize

Entry Deadline: 4/30/2021
Entry Fee: $25
Prize: $1,000

Berkshire Prize for a First or Second Book of Poetry

Entry Deadline: 4/30/2021
Entry Fee: $28
Prize: $3,000

Redivider's Beacon Street Prize

Entry Deadline: 4/30/2021
Entry Fee: $15
Prize: $500

Nimrod Literary Awards

Entry Deadline: 4/30/2021
Entry Fee: $20
Prize: $2,000

The 2021 Agnes Lynch Starrett Poetry Prize Competition
Entry Deadline: 4/30/2021
Entry Fee: $25
Prize: $5,000

Willow Books Literature Awards
Entry Deadline: 4/30/2021
Entry Fee: $30
Prize: $1,000

Noemi Press Book Awards
Entry Deadline: 4/30/2021
Entry Fee: $25
Prize: $1,000

The Richard Snyder Memorial Publication Prize
Entry Deadline: 4/30/2021
Entry Fee: $27
Prize: $1,000

May Poetry Contests

Tupelo Quarterly Poetry Prize
Entry Deadline: 5/1/2021
Entry Fee: $20
Prize: $500

The Poetry of the Sacred Contest
Entry Deadline: 5/1/2021
Entry Fee: $15
Prize: $500

Stan and Tom Wick Poetry Prize

Entry Deadline: 5/1/2021
Entry Fee: $30
Prize: $2,500

Moon City Poetry Award
Entry Deadline: 5/1/2021
Entry Fee: $25
Prize: $1,000

Fugue's Annual Writing Contest
Entry Deadline: 5/1/2021
Entry Fee: $15
Prize: $1,000

The Peseroff Prize
Entry Deadline: 5/1/2021
Entry Fee: $10
Prize: $1,000

Janet B. McCabe Poetry Prize
Entry Deadline: 5/5/2021
Entry Fee: $20
Prize: $1,500

The Idaho Prize
Entry Deadline: 5/15/2021
Entry Fee: $25
Prize: $1,000

Loraine Williams Poetry Prize
Entry Deadline: 5/15/2021
Entry Fee: $15
Prize: $1,000

Robert Dana-Anhinga Prize for Poetry
Entry Deadline: 5/15/2021
Entry Fee: $28
Prize: $2,000

Crab Creek Review Poetry Prize

Entry Deadline: 5/15/2021
Entry Fee: $16
Prize: $500

Ploughshares Emerging Writer's Contest
Entry Deadline: 5/15/2021
Entry Fee: $24
Prize: $1,000

Blue Lynx Prize for Poetry
Entry Deadline: 5/15/2021
Entry Fee: $28
Prize: $2,000

BorderSenses Poetry Contest
Entry Deadline: 5/15/2021
Entry Fee: $10
Prize: $250

Gertrude Press Chapbook Competition
Entry Deadline: 5/15/2021
Entry Fee: $17
Prize: $250

The Backwaters Prize
Entry Deadline: 5/31/2021
Entry Fee: $25
Prize: $1,000

Black River Chapbook Competition
Entry Deadline: 5/31/2021
Entry Fee: $15
Prize: $500

Grist's Pro Forma Writing Contest
Entry Deadline: 5/31/2021
Entry Fee: $18
Prize: $750

Tethered by Letters 2021 Spring Literary Contest

Entry Deadline: 5/31/2021
Entry Fee: $8/poem
Prize: $300

Juxtaprose 2021 Poetry Contest
Entry Deadline: 5/31/2021
Entry Fee: $15
Prize: $500

The Cossack Review's October Poetry Prize
Entry Deadline: 5/31/2021
Entry Fee: $15
Prize: $400

June Poetry Contests

Boston Review Annual Poetry Contest
Entry Deadline: 6/1/2021
Entry Fee: $20
Prize: $1,500

2021 TIFERET Writing Contest
Entry Deadline: 6/1/2021
Entry Fee: $15
Prize: $1,500

Boulevard Emerging Poets Contest
Entry Deadline: 6/1/2021
Entry Fee: $15
Prize: $1,000

The Bitter Oleander Press Library of Poetry Award
Entry Deadline: 6/15/2021
Entry Fee: $25
Prize: $1,000

Guy Owen Award
Entry Deadline: 6/15/2021
Entry Fee: $20
Prize: $1,000

Akron Poetry Prize

Entry Deadline: 6/15/2021
Entry Fee: $25
Prize: $1,500

Annual Gival Press Oscar Wilde Award

Entry Deadline: 6/27/2021
Entry Fee: $5
Prize: $100

May Sarton New Hampshire Poetry Prize

Entry Deadline: 6/30/2021
Entry Fee: $25
Prize: $1,000

New Measure Poetry Prize

Entry Deadline: 6/30/2021
Entry Fee: $28
Prize: $1,000

Barrow Street Book Contest

Entry Deadline: 6/30/2021
Entry Fee: $28
Prize: $1,000

Cider Press Editors' Prize

Entry Deadline: 6/30/2021
Entry Fee: $25
Prize: $1,000

The Autumn House Press Contests

Entry Deadline: 6/30/2021
Entry Fee: $30
Prize: $2,500

July Poetry Contests

Bellevue Literary Review Prizes

Entry Deadline: 7/1/2021
Entry Fee: $20
Prize: $1,000

Auburn Witness Poetry Prize
Entry Deadline: 7/15/2021
Entry Fee: $15
Prize: $1,000

Vallum Award for Poetry
Entry Deadline: 7/15/2021
Entry Fee: $25
Prize: $750

Rattle Poetry Prize
Entry Deadline: 7/15/2021
Entry Fee: $20
Prize: $10,000

Dream Quest One Poetry Contest
Entry Deadline: 7/31/2021
Entry Fee: $5
Prize: $250

Red Paint Hill Byant-Lisembee Book Prize (Poetry)
Entry Deadline: 7/31/2021
Entry Fee: $20
Prize: $300

New Millenium Writings Poetry Contest
Entry Deadline: 7/31/2021
Entry Fee: $20
Prize: $1,000

BOATT Poetry Chapbook Competition
Entry Deadline: 7/31/2021
Entry Fee: $14
Prize: $500

Seattle Review Poetry Chapbook Contest

Entry Deadline: 7/31/2021
Entry Fee: $20
Prize: $1,000

August Poetry Contests

Makeda Bilqis Literary Awards
Entry   Deadline: 8/15/2021
Entry   Fee: $12
Prize: $100

The Brighthorse Prize
Entry   Deadline: 8/16/2021
Entry   Fee: $25
Prize: $1,000

The New Guard Contest in Poetry
Entry   Deadline: 8/20/2021
Entry   Fee: $20
Prize: $1,500

September Poetry Contests

Patricia Dobler Poetry Award
Entry Deadline: 9/5/2021
Entry Fee: $20
Prize: $1,000

Los Gatos Poetry Contest
Entry Deadline: 9/10/2021
Entry Fee: $10
Prize: $600

Miller Williams Poetry Prize
Entry Deadline: 9/30/2021
Entry Fee: $28
Prize: $5,000

Tom Howard/Margaret Reid Poetry Contest

Entry Deadline: 9/30/2021
Entry Fee: $10
Prize: $1,500

October Poetry Contests

The Jake Adam York Prize
Entry Deadline: 10/15/2021
Entry Fee: $25
Prize: $2,000

James Hearst Poetry Prize
Entry Deadline: 10/31/2021
Entry Fee: $20
Prize: $1,000

Rhino Poetry Founders' Prize
Entry Deadline: 10/31/2021
Entry Fee: $10
Prize: $500

November Poetry Contests

Tethered By Letters Fall Poetry Contest
Entry Deadline: 11/1/2021
Entry Fee: $8
Prize: $300

December Poetry Contests

Annual Gival Press Poetry Award
Entry Deadline: 12/15/2021
Entry Fee: $20
Prize: $1,000

Jeff Marks Memorial Poetry Prize
Entry Deadline: 12/15/2021
Entry Fee: $20
Prize: $1,000

SONGWRITER CONTESTS

If you are a poet, you can become a lyricist. You may have to link up with a local guitar player, piano player or music teacher to develop the melody if the contest has a requirement for both.

American Songwriter has periodic contests with awards culminating in an annual contest with awards. Their period contests are for just lyrics with a cash award of $500 every couple of months The deadline this year for their big contest is for both lyrics and melody combined and performed in the entry. The closing date is December 1, 2021. There is an entry fee.

1ˢᵗ **Prize:** Cash award of $10,000, co-publishing contract offer with LiveXLive Music Publishing, and 2-page feature spread in American Songwriter magazine.

2ⁿᵈ **Prize:** Cash award of $1,000, one-page feature in American Songwriter and lifetime membership.

3rd **Prize:** Cash award of $500, one page feature in American Songwriter and lifetime membership.

I gave you this contest, since only lyrics are required for their periodic contests and poets can win that $500 prize just by sending in their written material. There are many great songwriting contests out there with high cash awards, but the ones I reviewed want the melodies to accompany the lyrics and often a performance that is not judged on the performer, but on the lyrics and melody only.

For those of you musically inclined as well as poetically proficient, here is a list of some of the major contests I found on GEMTRACKS that also included the American Songwriter Contest:

- The Chris Austin Songwriting Contest
- Songdoor International Songwriting Competition
- Guitar Center Singer-Songwriter Contest
- The USA Songwriting Competition
- Nashville Song Writers Association International Song Writing Contest
- Mountain Stage Newsong Contest
- Mid-Atlantic Song Contest
- The John Lennon Songwriting Contest
- International Songwriting Competition
- Great American Song Contest

I did leave out the Pulitzer Prize and Nobel Prize. Feel free to consult their websites for submission requirements. I know the Pulitzer Prize cash award is $15,000 annually.

BLOG

CHAPTER 7

BLOGGING

Blogging is a great low cost way to invade the Internet space with interesting poems and information about them and the blogger. Those that become adept can begin making money by providing ads from companies that pay per click on their ad placed on the blog.

Some of the best blogs bring in hundreds of thousands of dollars. Some of the blogs are free to install; however, they still have to be placed on a blogging/website host platform and that is where the cost is determined with payment plans available by the month, year or multiyear.

BLOGGING CRITERIA

Before conducting a search for the best top rated platforms pertinent to writers and poets, we should have some criteria for our search and keep those factors in mind while searching for the one that makes the most sense to us financially, visually and physically.

Blogging Tools We Must Have

I must admit I am searching for the best blogging platform myself. I am not an expert in this field, but I have to learn as much as you, because I want to begin blogging. We are on a journey together. Hopefully my research will help me make a decision and contribute to your decision making process. I will be looking for "Bests" in all blogging tool categories, but recognize there may be tradeoffs, because I do not want to pay an arm and a leg for my blogging platform.

Simplicity and Structure (Design)

Some blogging hosts have a series of templates; in some cases more than 1,000. I cannot imagine being that picky, because I can be content with constructing a beautiful page with only a few templates. Many offer more than 100 templates. Number of templates is certainly not a deal breaker for me. I trust in my sense of color, font usage, photo enhancements and the other simple tools. The page must be inviting to every reader.

TIP: Do not discount the importance of "white space." One can pack too much into the opening page and lose the interest of the audience.

SSL Security and Spam Protection

This is your security blanket. It comes with SSL Certification. Search engines now will avoid any site without them, as will computer virus programs and label such site without SSL Certification as "risky." Only the stupid would click into a "risky" site.

Apparently blogs make great places for spammers to attempt to penetrate. This is another thing I learned in the process. You need protection from visitors simply wanting to spam your blog or hack into it for cybercriminal activities. The most targeted weakness is the Comments section. Another set of visitors want to post irrelevant comments, or link their spam on your blog back to their own sites to give themselves a higher ranking. You could lose your traffic and even the blog. There are four cures for this and it may require all four:

1. On/Off Comment Button: If you are receiving

little value from site users, you want the capability to turn off the comments. That will depend on the blogging platform, so add that into your wish list of features.

2. Comment Monitoring: Depending on the platform one can monitor the comments before approving them to go public. This assures only the valid relevant ones get through to the public. It may require a lot of time on a busy site, but it might be worth the effort, rather than simply turning off the comments system.

3. Install Anti-Spam Tools: You can add "plugin" tools to your site to eliminate spam. These protection systems check the comments and submissions to other places like you're your contact form and prevent the blog from publishing the content.

4. Spam Blacklisting: If there is a continual flow of spam from one IP address, you want the ability to blacklist the users and the IP address, just as you do on emails.

System Navigation Menu: Since I have a website, I can imagine having the simplicity of drag and drop capability. What am I dragging and dropping? I am dragging a title from the tool box over to where I wish to place it on the site and then unclick to drop it in place. I type in the title, perhaps making it all capital letters in red. I can do the same with a location for a picture and then upload the picture from my computer. Then I can adjust the size of the picture and push it around to where I really want it to end up.

Usually you as the blogger have the ability to establish the navigation menu. Please do it on your homepage for all to see. The criteria for you doing this are:

1. Functional and Responsive.

2. Consistent Location of the Buttons.

3. Simplicity. Less is better. Limit the options.

4. Visibility. I really do not like searching for the buttons, only to find out that there are click on names at the bottom of the homepage. What a waste of my time. If there would be too many buttons on the top, by all means add the extra ones at the bottom, but prioritize for the top ones.

5. Logical Navigation. TIP: Do not confuse the visitor. For example, make sure the "Contact" button does not take them to the "About Me" page.

SEO Tools

Search Engine Optimization (SEO) tools are designed to provide information in millisecond speed when someone enters a search engine title, word, or phrase. That accounts for the order of the material presented up front for the viewer to click and receive the first feeds. SEO can make or break a site by where they locate your information and summary. I sometimes notice at the top of a search engine when I enter the information I am seeking in order a number like 8 million more with that title, word, or phrase. I could spend the rest of my life searching one item.

Social Media Integration

I never realized I could integrate my blog with social media platforms to expand my blogging network. Having a link to my blog on social media platforms allows more people to get updates and to visit my blog. That much I knew, but I did not know I could make one post to all my social media accounts simultaneously. This is accomplished in three ways:

1. Social Share Button: A social share button can be included on you blog. Visitors can click on that button and share the blog's content on their own platform from you, thus widening your target audience.

2. Social Login: If you wish greater security of your content, there is a method to require visitors to register, or sign up first prior to accessing content. To do this, the latest method is for visitors to simply use their social media accounts to register or log in. That makes it fast and easy and does not require the visitor to come with a new user name and horrors, another password. Statistics found on the Internet show this is by far the preferred method of logging onto a blog or website secured in this way.

3. Social Media Feeds: There is a method to embed social media feeds on your blog. This makes it more interactive by using a hashtag relevant to your topic and have social media posts running through the feeds on the blog.

Search Box

Initially there is nothing for which to search, but over time this function becomes more important as a reader may remember a particular poem you wrote and try to find it. I have learned to use "Search" now when I want to find one of my poems on my own word processing storage. I have written too many poems to remember where I put it.

System for Commenting

Commenting can get dicey, but it makes the reader feel involved. You may receive not only complements, but ideas from the readers. The downside is you may also acquire detractors, debaters, and other nonessential communicators and want to shut off, or delete comments. Control of this function yourself is the key.

Section for Archives

Ability to archive requires storage capability of the site. These come in megabytes or gigabytes of storage. As a poet of any description you likely do not require a fantastic amount of storage, so you may be able to compromise here and pay less in the process..

Site Summary Feed

This is known as "RDF Site Summary, and also Really Simple Syndication" abbreviated RSS. That is how the web and web audience receive updates from their favorite websites and blogs. With RSS, your intrepid readers get notified whenever a new post goes out from your site, since a brief summary is provided. Think of the search engine pages that have the descriptions with a clickable link above it. The receptor or casual search engine reader can read the summary of the post, or at least the beginning paragraph and two and decide whether they want to go to the site immediately. For those unfamiliar with your site, it is the enticement, or temptation factor. See if the site has an RSS feed. If it does, you'll usually find a button that looks something like this: , or you may simply see RSS. You will want to use RSS to promote your blog and grow your community of followers.

Strategic Internal Linking

I added the word "Strategic" to the industry standard known as internal linking. That is because I do not want to interrupt the reader unintentionally, but at strategic pauses that I deduce offer the best time for the linking. Some of the internal links are like footnotes, because they will say, "See my poem XXX." The reader has the option of going to that poem should they so desire.

Scheduling Button

Among the many things I did not realize is that one can write a blog, then set a date and time for it to go out with the proper tool. I was thinking I had to sit down on an exact date, prepare the information and send it then. Scheduling allow me to prepare a blog anytime during a week (my planned blogging interval) and have it automatically sent! Who knew?

Special Category Bar

These are the bars with buttons or clickable words seen at the top, bottom, or both that provide connections to the usual categories we see such as About the Author, Contact the Author, Poem Archive, and whatever we deem the most important categories for our blog. We want the bar to be well organized and to cover our needs.

Wow! Do you realize I just employed the Letter "S" for all twelve blogging tools! No, not the ten I just listed under Social Media Integration, but the entire foregoing package. The industry will likely take a dim view of it, but it helped me to get a fix on what is important.

FIVE MORE FACTORS BEYOND THE TOOLS

Most of the things we want and need for blogging come from the tools provided by the site host, or acquired from a source and embedded.

Support

We would like to find 24/7 support with a live body technically proficient to answer our questions quickly and solve problems. This support varies to some extent from one provider to the next as we shall see.

Site Hosting

I am going to give you information about twelve site hosts and my analysis derived from several source on the Internet of their capabilities and benefits.

Call-To-Action Buttons

Internet people think they invented the "Call-to-Acton." For their information that is a primary marketing tool. What is it you are selling? For poets it is their masterpieces lodged in books and chapbooks. You will want a direct link to the location on the sales and marketing platform where they may purchase it and all the other things you have written. Here are some categories for the "CTA" buttons: 1.) Submit. 2.) Enter. 3.) Subscribe. 4.) Buy Now. and 5. Checkout, if you are selling directly from your site. I suspect there is little need for that, since most books are available on sales and marketing platforms. You just need to link them with your site.

Contact Methods

How much tolerance do you have with the public and how much privacy are you willing to surrender? Readers often would like to have a way to contact you. Here are some ways: 1.) Provide a social media address where they can find you and message you. This means you may start getting a lot of new "Friends." 2.) A Contact Form. 3.) Third-party form builder. 4.) Email address. 5.) Telephone Contact Number.

Author Bio

If a reader is interested in your blog and the information contained therein, it stands to reason they will take an interest in the source of all that wonderful information, news, poems, and desiderata. Construct an easy to read bio and place it on your "About Me" button.

BLOGGING PLATFORMS

Here are twelve of the best blog sites that are presently available in 2021:

- Blogger
- Ghost
- Medium.com
- Postach.io
- Site123
- Squarespace
- Tumblr.com
- Typepad.com

- Weebly
- Wix
- WordPress.org
- WordPress.com

Blogger

Blogger is owned by Google, so it has Google ap integration and Google storage for images and files with 15 GB of free space. For those boycotting Google, this is not the platform for you. Since this is a Google captive platform, it is subjected to Google ads.

1. Features: The advantages are ease of use for newcomers to blogging and they have an impressive selection of templates that include versions for mobile users optimized for smaller screens. Blogger is web responsive. Blogger tool bars are simple ones. They have a spam filter and you can monitor comments on the dashboard and see visitor statistics including a visual world map of your global reach to readers internationally. Support is via the Blogger user forum, which is less than optimal. As a free blogging site though, courtesy of Google ads, it is an excellent choice for beginners.

2. Cost: Free.

Ghost

Ghost is an open-source blogging platform that is listed on some rating sites as the best alternative to WordPress. When the platform came online, it was meant primarily for journalists, editors and **writers**.

1. Features: Ghost places you in control of your blog design with no rules on customizations, or social media restrictions. You can even monetize your site, but you have to be on one of their premium plans. There is an impressive array of tools that are perfect for professionals who seek complete site control. These tools are not for the novice, since they include coding and additional functionality using high technology. I have an inkling this is a little too much management and technical learning required of writers.

1.) The Site Editor creates and embeds media files. 2.) You have complete management control of content. 3.) Scheduling provides the posts by your editorial schedule. 4.) The SEO tools are world class with comprehensive SEO features for high rankings on search engines. Templates are regarded as simple and "stunning. 5.) Automatic backup.

2. Cost: After a free 14-day trial the Basic Plan is $29 per month billed for a year as one single up front payment of $348. The Standard Plan is $79/month payable up front for the year as $948.

Medium

This is considered another simple platform, and it was specifically designed **for writers.** Their no-frills, no nonsense content publishing lets bloggers write their passions without the technical worries of codes, designs, domains, or other issues.

1. Features: No-frills means just that. There are not many benefits and you are captive to the Medium Partner Program for avid readers willing to pay for quality content.

That is the way to monetize your Medium blog posts, although your blog does go out to the world. If you create quality content that follows Medium guidelines, you can share your content with the editorial board who then check for adherence to their standards. If you pass, you can start earning money by attracting subscribers. Key Features: 1.) Access to a vast audience of site readers through subscriptions. 2.) Fee mobile ap.. 3.) Monetization. 4.) Social media integration. 5.) Media embeds permitted.

Cost: Free, although they have begun a subscription program. They have a membership program for $50 a year that allows you to subscribe for unlimited access to the brightest writers and biggest ideas on Medium. That sounds to me rather like an elite club.

Postach.io

To get an account with Postach.io, you must sign up with Evernote, install Evernote and then integrate it with Postach.io. Users then are able to use the dashboard to personalize website, but then write blogs with Evernote.

1. Features: The features that come with joining Postachi.io and Evernote are 1.) Allowance to insert pictures including a personal one or avatar. 2.) Synchronization with Evernote. 3.) A site editor with strong dashboard. 4.) Custom, but payment for a domain.

Cost: You can set up a free blog with this software, but if you want a custom domain, subscribe to a paid package. Postach.io also offers a collection of free and premium themes to help you create a visually appealing blog.

The free blog is useable without showing a credit card. The step up plan for 1-5 sites is $50 annually.

Site 123

Site 123 is regarded as one of the best free blogging platforms and from which one can build a small business website, or even eCommerce website employing only a few clicks.

1. Features: 1.) Ease of building a blog site. 2.) SEO tools with considerable power for optimizing a blog. 3.) Responsive and flexible web designing with mobile friendly website. 4.) More than 350 design templates. 5.) Visually pleasing and perfect for many industries.

2. Cost: Free with payment for addons as do most free sites.

Squarespace

In reality Squarespace is a drag-and-drop website builder aimed at small business enterprise owners, but these features also make it an ideal all-in-one solution for those of us with limited technical knowledge who want to establish a blog.

1. **Features:** Squarespace offers hosting, domain registration and the potential for eCommerce. 1.) Simple to use and beginner friendly. 2.) Professional design templates offered. 3.) SSL encryption built into the platform. 4.) Store

building capability. 5.) Free trial period to test the platform. 6.) Hosting. 7.) Custom domain. 8.) 24/7 support.

2. Cons: 1.) Limited to Squarespace features. 2.) Integrates only with selected third-party service and tools. 3.) Personal plan limitation of 20 pages. 4.) Overpowered for a simple blog. 4.) When people reblog your content, they have the right to modify it. 5.) Limited Customization.

3. Cost: Monthly cost for the Personal Plan is $12/month. If you make an annual payment, then you also get a discount and free custom domain. Included is unlimited pages, unlimited bandwidth and storage. You have a 14-day trial period.

Tumblr

Yes, that Tumblr. Their main focus is on multimedia and short-form content making it what is called in the industry a "microblogging" platform. If you intend more extensive writing and posting, Tumblr is not for you. That turned me off, as I suspect it did most of you. Writers need a more extensive permissive platform. Since it is used more as a social network cite you have the normal integration of limited writing space with photos, videos, and audio files. Tumblr is a mixed social media and blogging site that appeals to the 18-25 year-old category.

1. Features: 1.) Tumblr is a global site visited by millions daily who repost their favorite blogs and initiate conversations. 2.) Custom domains composed of 64 characters or less. 3.) ZIP file exporting. 4.) Password protection. 5.) Customized themes with anything you envision. 6.) Social Media Integration, of course, with other social platforms. 7.) You can build a following through the platform. 8.) There are ways to monetize your blog.

2. Cons: You do not own your site or content. That can be a deal breaker.

3. Cost: Free including a subdomain such as blogname.tumblr.com.

TypePad

TypePad.com is highly regard for businesses and writers with a simple user-friendly interface and exceptional customer support.

1. Features: 1.) Fully Hosted, so no software worries. 2.) Great variety of design tools. 3.) Flexible publishing from any device. 3.) Google Analytics Integration to study audience engagement. 4.) Theme builder from scratch. 5.) Beautiful templates. 6.) All the built-in tools to get noticed on social networks and by search engine rankings.

2. Cost: Free trial period only, then select one of four plans all billed month-to-month. Plus-$8.95/Unlimited-$14.95/Premium-$29.95/Enterprise-$49.95.

Weebly

Weebly is the ultimate drag-and-drop tool site that allows you to choose the elements to add to the site and flexibility of placement. By default Weebly became my website builder and maintainer, but it came to me through one of the other platforms mentioned here. I suppose the site I used had farmed it out. Furthermore, although I can keep Weebly and continue to input to the site, the platform I used changed their system in January 2021 and no longer provides their own support for the application.

1. Features: 1.) Eliminates messing around with menus. 2.) Place content blocks in predetermined areas which some may find limiting. 3.) 500 MB of storage. 4.) Template selection. 5.) There is a secret draft link that lets you preview your unpublished post and even share with friends prior to release. 6.) There is an area for pasting in Google Analytics tracking code. 7.) Weebly places an unobtrusive ad in the footer of your site.

2. Cost: Starter Package - $5 a month, Weebly Pro - $12 a month, Business - $25 a month.

Wix

Wix has a "highly intuitive" editor with outstanding flexibility in blog design. With the free package your site will have Wix branding with limits of 500 MB storage and a limit of 500 MB of data transfer per month.

1. Features: 1.) Unlimited number of pages. 2.) Powerful blog functionality. 3.) Simple editing, but access to image galleries, videos and music, plus a an amazing number of ways to customize your blog. 4.) Flexibility in post scheduling with the trick of automatically pushing it to Facebook when published. 5.) Artificial Design Intelligence Editor that asks basic questions and then quickly produces something close to what you envisioned. 6.) Quality customer support even on the free plan. 7.) Wix Turbo feature that increases speed and performance.

2. Cost: Free for lowest level, Connect Domain - $3.54 a month/Wix Combo - $14 a month/Wix Pro - $23 a month.

WordPress.org

I gleaned from online sources that WordPress.org, is NOT to be confused with WordPress.com. WordPress.org is far and away the most popular blogging platform in the world, powering over 90% of all Internet blogs. They are also the best for self-hosted blogs. They are for the serious blogger from the individual to full online businesses.

1. Features: WordPress.org is designed for those seeking full control over their site. 1.) Highly flexible. 2.) Complete site control. 3.) Over 55,000 plugins through their directory. 4.) Thousands of mobile-friendly themes with instant switching of the design depending on the audience you want to reach. 5.) Search engine and social media friendly. 6.) Complete ownership of content. 7.) Powerful support.

2. Cons: You still have to get web hosting and domain name.

3. Cost: Free to use as an open-source blogging platform, but $10 a year for domain name and $4 a month for web hosting. They make their money off the premium plugins and themes that add to platform flexibility.

4. Note: To get started you need to choose a web host offering one click installation for WordPress.org and follow the guide for how to start a blog.

WordPress.org sounds like it has a lot of features I may not need as a writer, but if I were searching to begin again, I would look into it.

WordPress.com

WordPress.com also has advanced features and extensive plugins offered. It is called a "brilliant" platform for bloggers at any level of experience and technological capability. Creating your first blog makes use of a relatively simple wizard that guides you through a series of choice like name and theme. After following the wizard's guidance, you may immediately begin posting. Advanced features and plugins are offered. The advanced editor allows you to customize your entire blog's appearance. They are not drag-and-drop, so you have to familiarize yourself with the series of menus, but in the long run you have established a highly personalized blog. The editor includes pages like an author bio.

1. **Features:** The writing interface resembles a desktop word processor and offers a wide range of customizable tools. They provide: 1.) Flexibility. 2.) Ease of use. 3.) Customizable social media sharing buttons. 4.) Geotagging permits finding worldwide locations of readers. 5.) Tracking statistics by view, number of visitors and comments. 6.) Hosting on WordPress.com servers. 7.) Privacy protection is extended to domains registered through wordpress.com.

2. **Cons:** 1.) With the free service there is no email or live chat support, but the community forum works well. 2.) WordPress.com displays ads on free blogs.

3. **Cost:** Free and then payment for additional features.

BLOGGING FOR FUN AND PROFIT

Now let us suppose you have installed a blogging platform and are ready to input information (text, photos, video, ads). The first thing I would do is look at blogs online of other people to gain some ideas of the template you wish to use and how to structure your own blog. I am not talking about imitation, although that may work very well for you, but let your creative juices to flow to make it have a personality of its own, just like a mirror of you. Don't like what you see in the mirror? Consult your alter ego, a friend, find a consultant online, anybody, but a relative.

Structure

1. Consistency: Begin with a structure that you will use repetitively. Why? The audience must identify with you immediately upon clicking into your blog. They seek familiarity. They all have trust issues, so the more consistent the blog, the more trust they will accord to your site and indirectly to you.

2. Organization: A disorganized display is the last thing you want to present your case as a cultured classical poet, or anyone else for that matter. That is another trust issue that must be cultivated by organizing the data and information. If the site is disorganized your audience will give up on you as quickly as it takes them to click out of your blog or website. Having a structure that is readable, shareable, perusable, and useful is paramount to attracting readers along with the beauty of the site.

As with everything in this Guide, what I am giving you is

suggestions that I hope you will take to heart. Nothing is mandatory (except the serif font), but in a poetry writer structure here is what I recommend:

1. Focus on the Introduction: We all know the saying about first impressions mattering most. In an impersonal digital online word, first impressions are even more important to attract readership. You want to delight the reader and grab their attention. Insert something as a hook on which they can hang their hat and stay awhile.

You may ask me, "How do I do that?" My answer differs from all the recent material I have read that simply throw it into a common basket I do not like.

The suggestions from others go like this: 1.) Ask a question. 2.) Provide an eye-catching statistic. 3.) Tell a story. Nooo!

I despise having a question thrown at me in the introduction, or initial text. (I also don't like the word, "Introductions.") I am thinking, do I have to answer it; why was the question asked in the first place; will the author give me the answer now or later, if you don't know, how should I know the answer? You will also have noted by now I do not like lettered subheads like A, B,C. Let us think like the writer of a novel. How about this one, "It was the best of times; it was the worst of times." Did that pique my interest? Yes, it did, and I was only in high school at the time I read Charles Dickens' novel, "A Tale of Two Cities." That example gives me my first recommended approach, a catchy phrase that makes me want to read more. A blog to me is like writing a short story and I need something with immediate impact. What I am saying is applicable to all writers, however, I will continue to show evidence of focusing on poets for the purpose of this book.

Here is my short list of how I would like to start my own blog and book as well:

- Catchy phrase
- Challenging Statement
- Conundrum
- Eloquent Statement
- Humor
- My Best Poem
- Pithy Quote
- Satire
- Vision of Something
- Warning (Reading this may be dangerous to your friend's health!)
- Words of Wisdom

As book agents will tell you, begin with something that draws the reader into what you have to present, pique their interest, and make them hunger for more. (These are my own words, but I have found related verbiage in sample rejection notices.) I am sure you will come up with your own "hook," but I offer these ideas listed above for your use. Your final sentence should provide a smooth transition to the rest of the blog, or book, if you will.

2. The Substance: I do not like the word "Body," either. We all learned it in school, but it felt like I was literally doing something to a body. The first replacement I typed for the heading was "Meat," but then I worried about vegans out there You never know about classical poets, or modern free verse poets for that matter. I decided that "Substance" was sufficiently neutral, so I went with that word. Substance is where my English teacher mother's instruction on writing once again comes into play. Time to make an outline.

There are several ideas, concepts, points, or call it what you will that I want my reader to consider with examples thrown in purposefully. The Outline, like my Table of Contents, provides one major idea at a time condensed into logical headings and subheadings. Some of the novels I read are "wall-to-wall" texts that take the joy out of reading. I may need to take a break to get a cup of coffee and lose my place. You may use numbers and alphabetical letters, if you wish, but it may distract the audience.

Depending on the subject matter, inject some enthusiasm and initiative into your writing so the reader does not fall asleep while reading it, or soon sign off. Your personality should come shining through. Technical blogs typically will not be inspired writing, but they can be entertaining. As a poet, you should have the ability to write as well in your blog, as you do your poetry, but then I haven't read your poetry.

3. Hail and Farewell: You may think of this as the conclusion, but you may not really be concluding anything, or wish it to end right there. Afterall, you want them to come back. Hail and Farewell seems to me a fairer assessment of the circumstance of ending one's particular blog, but inviting them to return again and again. You may want to project out to the subject of your next blog, or blogs. As a poet, you do want continual traffic on your site. You may not realize it, but there is a greater audience out there that may become your fans.

4. Referencing: See, I told you we were not through. I am glad I did not put Conclusion in the text. Now you can provide links to your book(s), website(s), blog(s), or anything else you believe the reader may like to see, especially since they made it this far. If you are selling something, this is also the time for a "Call to Action." That is the final marketing instruction you will get in a marketing class.

The Call to Action is heard everyday on television ads. Call now and get a discount. Call now and get free shipping. Call now, because you needed it yesterday!

Visual Content

I learned a long time ago that 65% of the population are visual learners. The other two categories are auditory (listening) and kinesthetic (hands on). Visual content is important not just for the 65%, but the others as well, since it enhances what you are telling them in your text. In this day and age of social media, we certainly know the importance of a picture, called a meme, for even getting people to read our postings.

Visual content in a blog includes infographics, tables, mastheads, personal photos, boxed off quotations, images of any kind (art, sculpture, illustration), slideshows and video. A word of caution on videos. Often they are too long for the hosting site and take away from concentration.

I recommend providing a link to a site like YouTube, or some other platform for them to see should they so desire.

Visual displays are also useful, if parsimoniously used in the Substance.

Clarity

Find a niche and concentrate on providing an interesting blog on that subject. Classical Poets should already have classical poetry as their niche. If they are interested in each presentation on a blog, or at least some of them, they will return. Within classical poetry you can then present any poems on subjects that fall within your interest and purview.

Continual presentations of similar material and information will be welcome by your newly captive readership. That is why you should include a comments section and even a contact capability along with a search feature once you have written a lot of material on your blog over time.

Quality Blogging

Blogging requires commitment to a schedule of updating and new presentations. The blog should not just sit there and neither should a website. A reader who becomes enamored wants to be entertained on a regular basis. If you do not provide at least a weekly insertion of solid value, they will soon get bored and not return. Remember the aphorism about a bird in the bush. Whatever you do, do not throw a bunch of things together daily just to get something out. Neither delay for weeks or months. It would be like starting over again trying to attract a new audience.

Internal Links

I already mentioned the links at the end, such as to one of your books on a retail website. I have never been a fan of sprinkling internal links throughout a manuscript, because they slow down my reading, and I don't like that. I still prefer at the end in the References. An internal link must have relevancy, such as a similar or related poem written and posted on your blog several months ago. Linking also helps with Search Engine Optimization (SEO), so it should be included in each blog.

Each poet needs to decide on the features such as ease of use, or beauty of final product along with costs involved. As a beginner, the best platform is less demanding to establish and easy to use with things like drag and drop tools that require no coding skills.

Every blog also requires a host. It is recommended that the poet's blog and the poet's website be the same site for ease of use and cost considerations. See Website Hosting below.

Once the blog is up and running, it requires continual posting. The best way to maintain the blog is to set aside a time at least once a week to update the blog.

HOSTING

Source: <u>Wikimedia Commons</u>

All structured data from the file and property namespaces is available under the Creative Commons CC0 License; all unstructured text is available under the Creative Commons Attribution-ShareAlike License.
Requirement: Provide the name of the creator.

By Drsaifu - Own work, CC BY-SA 4.0,
https://commons.wikimedia.org/w/index.php?curid=45128952

CHAPTER 8

SOCIAL AND WEB HOSTING PLATFORMS

REVIEWS

There are a great many companies that will improve marketing your book or chapbook for a relatively inexpensive price. These book review companies like BookBaby and OnlineBookClub.org will provide favorable and hopefully insightful reviews that you can use in your own marketing efforts and give an initial impetus to book sales. Since I have not used any of them as yet, I simply offer an example of one as insight into how one company has a stair-stepped plan depending on desire and finances to get your self-published book into the public eye.

OnlineBookClub.org offers four levels:

Level 1 Review, Cost $97: includes a review, one week featured status in their forum and entry into Book of the Year Contest. Average turnaround time is four (4) months.

Level 2 Review, Cost $148: includes a review, two week featured status and entry into Book of the Year Contest. Average turnaround time is three (3) months.

Level 3 Review, Cost $197: includes a review, one (1) month featured status, one week homepage link to the review and entry into Book of the Year Contest.

Level 4 Review, Cost $297: includes two (2) months featured status, two (2) week homepage link to the review and entry into Book of the Year Contest. The review is "guaranteed" to be by one of their top reviewers. Average turnaround time is one (1) month.

I provided this information for comparative purposes, not as a recommendation. I wonder at the comment on the Level 4 Review about the guarantee of one of their top reviewers. Does that mean the other reviewers are less than optimal>

SOCIAL PLATFORMS

Each social platform (Facebook, Instagram, Parler, Pinterest, Twitter, and others) has a marketing capability for a price. The same applies to magazines, book review sections of newspapers on weekends and any communications outlet including self published blogs. One can spend serious money if one has the resources and wishes to at least establish a name in the social media industry.

I can tell you Facebook has a marketing program in which you may get placed before thousands of viewers for a relatively low cost that you can control yourself by placing a dollar limit. You control expenditures and audiences.

WEBSITE HOSTING

A website is something all poets need. It provides a stationary Internet space to which all friends and potential customers have access and can read about each book and endeavor. From posting one poem at a time to book covers one can tell a story about their poetic journey.

If you thought finding a printer/publisher was complex, wait until you learn about webhosting. You have learned that you are now a publisher with a printing firm that can distribute and market for you. On the other hand, you learned that the author must become the publicist and driver of sales with their constant presence in all the right market places. Developing your website with a domain name is the first task to attacking the online market with your virtual store. That virtual store with your domain name must have a provider. That is where the Web Host comes into the picture.

Just as you would have to do with owning your own physical store or paying rent for space occupied, that is what you have to do with a Web Host. You are paying the host to lease server space for your new company. The process is the same: identify the location (host) for marketing, identify your store or corner of a store (domain name), pay the rent (lease), and decide what you are going to put in your store (blog, website).

Once you have accomplished those tasks you need to decide the space you need. The host provides the hardware space to store your web content and then provides the internet connections to access it. Think of it as the door. The storefront window is your homepage. That is the first visual display to greet the customers, so it is important to get it right.

These are my criteria for selecting a Web Host for not only poets, but writers in every genre. We all have the same things in common, sales through separate channels, desire to be parsimonious in our expenditures, ease of building a website (Most of us are not technicians), ability to design a website with flexibility in display and entry of pictures and information, security of the system, easy to operate control panel (dashboard), and customer service.

1. Cost to Host: This is an obvious category, but we each must determine the added services we may wish for and require past our paying for the domain name, the platform and security. Our goal while maximizing our abilities is to limit the costs to the lowest possible amount given, since we do not require excessive services or volume sales capability.

2. Ease of Using a Website Builder: We are looking for a builder that can accommodate our vision of what our website should resemble, or at least provide a template with which we can work to approximate a good image. Features such as drag-and drop-placement, ease of insertion of information, and a help feature are highly desired.

3. Ability to Design the Site: We want a site to match our personality, provide optimum display of our products, beautify our blogs, and communication effectively in writing and visually with those who choose to linger on our website. Since we are the builder of our site with the help of the host builder, we want it to be easy to design the site to match our vision.

4. Secure System: We must obtain an SSL Certificate. I say that because search engines, not to mention our own antivirus programs are programmed now to skip those websites not armed with one. They are considered risky and thus business is turned away. The top Web Hosts typically bundle the SSL Certification with the package provided at no extra cost, since their servers are expected to be equipped anyway with added security. I suppose you could say this is my second "mandatory" tip.

5. Control Panel: This is the dashboard that allows access to editing the website. The control panel should be easy to use from an intuitive perspective, logically organized, and with clear buttons and instructions.

6. Customer Service: As poets that sometimes are inspired after midnight, we are interested in 24/7 customer support from reliable people preferably located in the United States and not overseas. At least that is my desire. They must be technically adept. If they lack specific knowledge in an area of our concern, they must immediately pass us off to the right source of information and support assistance.

7. Speed and Performance: If you are like me I was thinking I don't need speed, just access. I was wrong! Why is speed important? It is a major ranking factor for search engines, such as Google that help elevate your website for reader attention. Think of it this way. The fastest horse wins the race, gets the rose blanket, extra oats and pays off the bettors better. In the case of Web Host speed, we already know in advance the winner in the race to the search engine finish line and our website, blog, or whatever takes a higher position in the listings on the search engine site.

Some of the raters of websites said that site speed "is one of the most critical aspects for choosing the best web host." (Source: Adam Enfroy, "27+ Best Web Hosting Services of 2021, May 21, 2021." < adamenfroy.com/best-web-hosting-services#) "Besides the ranking there are things like bounce rate, time on page and conversion rates," whatever all those things are.

Web Hosting Tip: As a poet who decided on self-publishing, you are not a high volume store. That is what you already have with your printer/publishing company, distributor, and marketing firm. You do not need a high volume sales site, because you will refer them to those other places. Thus you are looking for the most cost effective website provider and web hoster.

There are many types of Web hosting companies and plans, but I will reduce it mainly to shared hosting firms. That is the most affordable type of hosting, because you are sharing space like in a shopping mall, or a boutique.

Book self-publishers certainly do not need the mammoth business models for storage and marketing. the two downsides are limits on amount of storage bytes and slowdowns if there is high traffic volume.

Don't worry. I doubt if either will bother you for a long time. If you suddenly become a volume seller, you can switch plans with volume hosts if you placed yourself there initially, or you can migrant to another platform, sometimes within the same provider.

Perhaps you remember the graphic I provided in front of this Chapter with the big question mark and next to it Dedicated Hosting, Cloud Hosting, or Shared Hosting. You may want to look into Virtual Private Servers or Cloud Hosting, but I assure you they are considerably more expensive. Dedicated Hosting is by far the most expensive and is meant for ultra high traffic volume, high sales volume and data storage.

I am going to provide you the list of the top twelve companies that supply hosting services and then delve into each of them. Here are twelve of the top rated hosting sites in 2021 in alphabetical order;

- A2 Hosting
- Bluehost
- Dreamhost
- GoDaddy
- HostGator
- Hostinger
- InMotion Hosting
- Liquid Web
- iPage
- SiteGround
- WordPress.com
- WPEngine

A2 Hosting

1. Features: A2 Hosting has plans catered to a wide variety of needs and requirements. They provide easy site transfer and 24/7 support by phone, chat or email. They have an anytime money-back guarantee.

2. Speed: They are considered to be one of the fastest web hosts.

1. Cost: Starter offer is for $3.92 a month that becomes $7.99 per month. Total initial cost is $140.94.

Bluehost

1. Features: On some of the online raters,

Bluehost is number one for a variety or reasons, not the least of which is unlimited bandwidth to make your website "infinitely scalable," allowing for unimpeded future growth. Their customer support staff is extremely knowledgeable and they tout no issue will go unsolved. Bluehost offers many key features including free domain name registration and free SSL certificates for openers. Bluehost allows automatic WordPress installation, free website migration, unlimited websites and marketing tools.

2. Speed: Rated as good to excellent.

3. Cost: Their entry package is presently discounted to $3.95 per month for 36 months with domain, subdomains, 50 GB of storage and other features thrown into the mix. Total checkout cost is $142.20.

Dreamhost

1. Features: Dreamhost is another site offering a free domain name and 24/7 support. Their uptime guarantee is 100% and their money back guarantee is one of the longest at 97-days. All sites have an SSL certification and a WordPress firewall for added security. There are many other impressive features, but for us as poets they do not mean much, except they improve performance.

2. Speed: Among the best.

3. Cost: Although they are one of the least costly hosts their renewal fee is the same as their introductory offer $93.24 for 36 months. With that comes unlimited traffic and bandwith plus Wordpress pre-installed.

GoDaddy

1. Features: GoDaddy is one of the oldest web hosts. They have one-click installation for over 125 aps and guarantee 99.9% uptime. Their website builder is one of the best along with their other top tier services. You get a free domain name with an annual plan. GoDaddy serves mostly individuals and small businesses making them more ideal for poets seeking a Web Host. With an annual plan you receive a free domain name registration, tutorial video for beginners and 99.9% uptime.

2. Speed: Rated as good to excellent with 99.9% uptime which matches almost all the industry bests.

3. Cost: Their plans range from $5.99 to $89.99 per month. Their plans beyond Economy allow one to host unlimited sites. The host cost is $15 per month, but comes with limited storage. The starting plan is $3.66 a month and goes up after a period of time, but the Economy Plan charges $5.99 a month for 36 months.

HostGator

1. Features: HostGator is an easy to use, affordable web host with intuitive site building and an easy to use control panel. It has unmetered disk space and bandwidth for expansion and drag-and-drop website templates. One may add unlimited domains and will assist with free migrations in the first 30 days. They offer 24/7 customer support through phone, live chat and email. HostGator has three imaginatively name main plans: Hatchling, Baby and Business with appropriate additional features. Their money back guarantee is for 45-days.

2. Speed: Their speed is not the fastest, but better than average and their uptime also is better than the average at 99.98%.

3. Cost: HostGator's lowest level plan start at $2.78 per month on a 36 month plan making them among the least expensive. The total checkout cost when joining is $100.08.

Hostinger

1. Features: Hostinger is one of the top three in ratings on most sites with scalable hosting solutions and payment levels for websites requiring speed. The free templates and site builder are intuitive to use and popular. The dashboard is clean and they offer a free SSL certificate and domains.

The website builder literally has 1,000's of templates. They have a 30-day money back guarantee. According to those rating host sites, Hostinger is an excellent beginners host that helps you learn to build a free site with WordPress. Their support team usually responds in less than two minutes on live chat

2. Speed: Being one of the fastest web hosting providers and with a guaranteed uptime of 99.9 percent they have established a reliable reputation.

3. Cost: Speed and price are their calling card with a 2021 first tier plan discounted to $0.99 a month with four years of hosting at $47.52.

InMotion Hosting

1. Features: InMotion offers a variety of hosting plans with the normal tiered pricing. The have free domain registration or migration from other hosts. They have a money back guarantee for up to 90-days. They have additional security packages to weed out hackers. Working with WordPress you receive up to 20,000 monthly visitors, 40 GB of storage and unlimited emails.

2. Speed: Their speed optimization is rated at ten times faster than average shared plans.

3. Cost: They are rated as the lowest cost managed WordPress hosting service at $4.99 a month for 36 months with checkout cost of $179.64. Their money back guarantee is for 90-days.

iPage

1. Features: iPage has free domain registration for one year. Presently they offer 75% off all hosting plans. They have scalable bandwidth for future expansion and unlimited diskspace. They offer 24/7 phone and chat support. Their easy to use website tools are perfect for beginners. They have hundreds of templates that integrate with content management systems including WordPress.

Their website builder is limited to just six pages. However, they have hundreds of templates and themes and integrate with content management systems (CMS) like Joomla and WordPress. You get a free custom website, email address and $200 worth of free ad credits for use with search engines. Their features for a cheaper host is good with unlimited disk space, unlimited SQL databased and unmetered bandwidth.

2. Speed: Their speed is rated as slower than most of the other plans listed here.

3. Cost: Although they have a low price of $1.99 per month for 36 months, that jumps to higher renewal fees of $7.99 to $9.99. Total cost for the first three year checkout is $71.64.

Liquid Web

1. Features: Liquid Web guarantees 100% uptime with dedicated hosting. They also have 24/7 live technical support by phone, chat, or email. Their calling card is primarily for fully managed hosting services and they have the industry best 59-second guarantee for 24/7 customer support. There are six different hosting options to fit your needs.

2. Speed: Rated excellent.

3. Cost: For a new site their Managed WordPress hosting package begins at $19.33 a month for twelve months with a checkout total of $232. There is a present 50% off for six months.

SiteGround

1. Features: SiteGround takes pride in the best customer support 24/7 via chat with a virtual 100% uptime and excellent page load times.

2. Speed: Excellent.
3. Cost: Basic plans begin at $3.95 per month plus a $14.95 setup fee that includes SSL, daily backups, unmetered

traffic and up to 10,000 monthly visitors.

WordPress.com Hosting
(Do Not Confuse with WordPress.org)

Features: This is one of the most popular free hosting platforms offering a free subdomain under WordPress.com (yourwebsite name.wordpress.com). There are free templates for building your website with limited storage of 3 GB, which should be enough for all poets. The cost is reduced by them displaying ads on your website, but that can be upgraded to a paid plan to eliminate them. There are additional features like a custom domain name and other access features for a price. One review suggested that by the time these things are costed out, any of the "almost free" websites offer a better option.

Looking at their benefits ad, Wordpress.org Hosting is specifically optimized for WordPress with auto-updates and backup, "bulletproof security," super speed, 24/7 support, plus flexible and scalable capability up to "huge traffic." While the stripped down version for individual hosting lacks the greater depth capability of settings and themes, it should be sufficient for self-publishing purposes.

Speed: Speed is faster due to native integrations and expert support teams.

Cost: WordPress hosting can cost anywhere from $5 to 100 per month. Think in terms of the individual at the low end and big business at the high end.

WPEngine

Features: WP Engine has completely managed and integrated WordPress hosting with technology for faster loading of pages. There is a free automated site migration plugin and enterprise-grade network security. Their money back guarantee is for 60-days.

As one can imagine, there is a wide range of capabilities: free or paid for domain name, free or paid for SSL certificate, drag and drop site builder, length of subscriptions, ease of use, and creativity that each host provides. They also may provide a website separate from the blog. They all come with marketing tools that can cost a lot monthly or annually. Like blogging, a website should have continual updating and new materials.

Speed: Their focus is speed, security and scalability with managed hosting specifically built for WordPress sites.

Cost: They are rated best for professional enterprise hosting with a price of $31.50 monthly for their startup plan.

X-FACTOR, SALES

I saved the worst news for last. In an article titled, "The 10 Awful Truths about Book Publishing," (June 2020) Steven Piersanti, Senior Editor for Berrett-Koehler Publishers provided statistics to show that while publishing in general and particularly self-publishing exploded in recent years, citing a 264% increase in five years to nearly 1.7 million in 2018, book sales are stagnant.

"By 2019, the total number of (all) books published in the U.S. exceeded 4 million in that year alone…" That includes the fall of E-book sales. Furthermore, "The average U.S.

book is now selling less than 200 copies per year and less than 1,000 copies over its lifetime."

Here is an outline of the "awful truths" from the source above that you can read for yourself online:

1. Numbers Explosion: The number of books being published every year has exploded.

2. Stagnant Sales: Book sales are stagnant, despite the explosion of books published.

3. Book Market Shrinking: Despite the addition of e-Book sales and downloadable audio sales, overall book sales have shrunk.

4. Small Average Book Sales: Average book sales are shockingly small at 200 copies annually, and falling fast.

5. Less Than 1% Stocking: A book has far less than a 1% chance of being stocked in an average bookstore.

6. New Titles Less Likely to Sell: It is getting harder and harder every year to sell new titles.

7. Most Books Sold Locally: Most books today are selling only to the authors' and publishers' communities.

8. Authors Must Market Their Own Books: Most book marketing today is done by authors, not by publishers.

9. Books are Most New Products: No other industry has so many new product introductions.

10. Rapid Industry Change: The book publishing world is in a never-ending state of change.

SUMMARY AND FULL SPEED AHEAD

Poster: Utopia of Aerial Navigation, Romaneta & Company,
Paris, Circa 1900.

CHAPTER 9

SUMMARY OF APPLIED KNOWLEDGE

FORMATTING

Layout

The usual paper size for a poetry book is 6 inches by 9 inches.

Borders are a matter of taste, but side borders are superfluous and distracting.

Outlining

Poetry subjects form the basis of the outline.

The outline becomes my Table of Contents.

For pagination, I prefer to locate the page numbers at the bottom of the page in the center. Tastes vary, so put them anywhere you like.

Cover Design

Get licensing permission for any artwork after 1923, otherwise you could be charged with copyright infringement.

Use a cover creator application that allows importation of the art. Some cover creators have their own art file, but at least for mine it is too narrow and not nice enough.

Since tracking down the title, artist and date is difficult online, I recommend going to Wikimedia Commons and find either the piece of art in which you have an interest, or a comparable work of art or illustration.

Font Selection

Every major book publisher uses a font with serifs. Those are the little appendages to the end points of letters that make them appear more elegant. Baskerville, Book Antiqua, Garamond and Times New Roman are certainly among the best choices, although there could be others such as Palatino.

Indenting

I used a mix of not indenting paragraphs unless I numbered the paragraph. I hope I succeeded in at least being consistent in that regard.

Grammar and Punctuation

Grammar and punctuation is one of the point of departure between traditional and classical poets and modern free verse poets. The classical poet invariably with use traditional English grammar and punctuation they were taught in school. One variation is inventing new words based on the Latin or Greek root of the word they could have used, except it did not rhyme.

    1. Commas: Poets have a wide range of options regarding the use of commas. Classical poets tend to use a larger number of commas for pauses and effect that modern free verse poets who may not use any, as in the case of e.e.cummings, who also disdained periods, except apparently for his name initials.

2. Capitalization: Capitalization is also as flexible as commas with a debate even among classical poets of their use at the beginning of every line as in the traditional poems, or if the sentence continues from the previous line, then leaving the first letter of the first word uncapitalized. I happen to like the traditional method of Capitalizing the first word of every line. More than that, I like to capitalize some nouns in the middle of sentences for effect and emphasis.

4. One Space after a Period: The digital age settled the debate between one or two spaces from the end of the last sentence to the first word of the next sentence. When I learned typing and English back in the Dark Ages, I had to have two spaces. One space now is not only preferred, it is required.

5. Indentation Standard: Indenting poems may be done any way that please the writer from stair-stepping and centering each line to having the left indent the same for every line straight up and down.

6. Paragraphing Conventions: These mostly do not apply to poets, who keep their poems in verses, although some poets of either classical or modern persuasion do not separate their poems into one verse, but instead have a wall of one verse that intimidates the reader.

Art as Section Dividers

I told you and emphasize the way to stay out of trouble with copywrite infringement is to find paintings, sculptures, illustrations, photos, or any graphic medium that pre-date 1923. My own best source is Wikimedia Commons for common sharing licenses even for pictures of old art. This is a sharing platform normally with free use as long as there is a comment to the effect it is used as a common license under their terms.

The other options are to find clipart, pay a collector gallery, or go directly to the artist and request permission to use their art. This latter normally comes with a fee, but I have been successful in some case obtaining permission and free usage.

Cataloging and Dates

I recently cataloged my poems in alphabetical order, because I no longer could remember in which book I placed the poem. Now I can look it up quickly for reference and finding it. I recommend before you have a burgeoning list of poems, you make a catalog and keep it updated.

I like to place the date when I wrote or completed the poem in parentheses next to my name. My reasons are historic value and jogs to my memory.

Poet Notes

I gave you a list of reasons for providing poet notes at the bottom of poems. 1.) Credits for quotes and material. 2.) Explanations of something obscure. 3.) Explanation of my thoughts that may be misunderstood, or not understood at all. 4.) Reference to something of value like another poem that is related. Poets typically do not footnote, but I have found it useful to make notes both for myself and my readers. Besides making notes that credit another source for material you used keeps you out of trouble.

PRODUCTION AND QUALITY

Editing Tips

My primary editing tip is do not attempt to edit your poem, or especially your book one time through. Treat each element separately and edit only for that factor from a written list you keep, or from your memory. Keep these edits separate: 1.) Words. 2.) Grammar. 3.) Spacing. 4.) Headers. 5.) Table of Contents pagination. 6.) Front Matter. 7.) Indentation top and bottom/side to side.

Double Checking

The best way to make a final double or triple check is to have a print copy. This is a primary factor stated by editors as essential and I have found by practice I have a greater chance of locating errors on paper than I do on a computer screen. Therefore, request a proof copy before approving for final printing.

Pre-Publication and Logo

You are about to become a publisher, true, a self-publisher. There are two things you need before you begin the process. The first is a name for your company that can be arranged with DBA (Doing Business As) name and a logo for your new company. Almost all the self-publishing companies out there consider themselves the printer and not the publisher. Some exceptions are made for those to whom you pay a lot of money for production and distribution.

PRINTING AND PUBLICATION

Beware Printers That Take Advantage

There are a lot of companies out there to which you have to pay considerable money for them to print your book often without editors or any other resources applied to working with you. From the chart I provided, the least of those had a special for $875, followed by two at $1,299. Then the price jumped to around $2,000 and went as high as $6,000.

All you need is patience to learn the process, do it yourself and save a ton of money. That includes using templates for the text and cover for free.

Printer/Publisher Selection

I gave you all the criteria with the bells and whistles for selecting the best printer and/or publisher for your book. I recommend you research the ones you may have selected from the chapter dealing with them. There are so many options, but some are critical.

Main considerations for self-publishing are ease of self-production and self-editing, free printing or up front cost, marketing reach and costs of marketing, distribution to national and international markets, editing resources available internal to the printer/publisher, and royalties.

Post-Production Proof Copy

This looks like a second time I mention a proof copy, but after final printing request only one copy and use it as another proof for a post-publication edit. You will be surprised at what you find that needs correction.

Volume or Chapbook

Consider a Chapbook to be less than 60 poems and a volume to be over that number. With my company in order to get the title and my name on the spine, I need to go over 140 pages.

WRITERS AND WRITING

Writers and writing was an interlude between printing, publishing and marketing to give you a sense of how I operate and prepare my poems for publication. The reason I inserted it here was I did not want to color your thinking with how I approach writing poetry, but I thought it important to insert it prior to attempting market your product. In a sense what I said should help you feel confident going forward, or change your approach to get the best out of you.

MARKETING AND SALES

Blogging

As I indicated, I have yet to start blogging, but I plan to do so now that I understand from my research how it works. My choice will likely come from one of the twelve companies that I provided in the lists and analysis. Blogging has now become essential, especially for the marketing of poetry books, so I must add that to my quiver of arrows. I trust you will do the same. The process I am going to use is narrow down the field to the top three, go to their website and investigate each one thoroughly. I will ask them questions in the process that I may still have after reading my analyses and their site presentations.

Contests

The contest list I provided from Ardor was extensive, but they are not all the contest out there. For example, they missed the Society of Classical Poets contest that has a cash award of $1,000 to the annual winner.

Local Outlets

For poetry books as for most others, the local outlets are the most important, particularly for new authors. The concept is to build from the local base to the regional and then on to the national. Think outside the box to find opportunities in everything from a flea market to a high school reunion.

Reviews

If you can get a review from a noted poet, more power to you. In the absence of that capability, you can pay firms that have reviewers to ensure you have a good third-party review and recommendation. You can then include it with your next poem or book, or with your marketing materials. Third-party reviews are important, because they make it seems as though other approved of your poetry and are in essence recommending buying it.

Social Platforms

I purposely did not go into social platforms because the change so often and because all of you should be familiar with one or more of them by now. I can tell you Facebook has a marketing program in which you may get placed before thousands of viewers for a relatively low cost that you can control yourself by placing a dollar limit.

Website Hosting

I do have a website that I use to post my books. By pure chance it is one of the ones listed that I provided in the chapter on web hosting firms. The discounts offered vary greatly from month to month. Remember some of the free sites to join morph into ones you need pay over the long run. Some Internet analysts suggest that free websites are not worth it, because of so many limitations, but I believe you will find one suitable for any poet from a beginner to almost the pro level and be satisfied with it.

The main criteria for me from the list I provided includes, ease of intuitive building, security, SEO capability and price.

FULL SPEED AHEAD

I offer these insights into my recent explorations I believe improved my own poetry writing and experience. Remember I am NOT stating rules, but observations. While I may never achieve the status of being a great poet, at least I may be regarded as a contributor to the pleasure of poetry readers. We owe it to our readers to put our best "foot" forward.

To that end, read the outstanding series on how to write poetry provided by the Society of Classical Poets on their website, or purchase the book by Evan Mantyk, Dusty Grein, et.al., *How to Write Classical Poetry: A Guide to Forms, Techniques, and Meaning* published by the Society of Classical

Poets. If this essay helps you improve your poetry, or at least answers a question of two, then writing my observations and perceptions has been worth my effort.

ENDNOTES

Disclaimer: I know how to produce Footnotes and Endnotes accurately, but in this book I use my own system for ease of citing and finding,

Foreword

Mantyk, Evan, <u>et.al.</u> *How to Write Classical Poetry,* Society for
Classical Poets, 2018.

Chapter 1

Page 3: *BookBaby,* <u>bookbaby.com/poetry-book-printing</u>.

Page 9: Peterson, Roy E. *As the World Turns: Poetry by the
Fireside.* TriCrown Books, 2018.

Page 12: *A Totally Definitive Ranking of Fonts* by Claire Fallon,
7/28/2014, <u>huffpost.com/entry/font-ranking</u>.

Chapter 2

None.

Chapter 3

Page 34: "Royalties: The Seduction of Self-Publishing. The
Independent Publishing Magazine. February 13, 2015.
http://www.theindependentpublishingmagazine.com/2015/02/royalti
es-the-seduction-of-self-publishing.html

Tip Page 43: "2021 Self-Publishing Price Comparison,"
WritersWeekly, March 4, 2021.

Chart Page 44, <u>Ibid</u>.

Chapter 4

None.

Chapter 5

None.

Chapter 6

Page 60: *Winning Writers, <adam@winningwriters.*

Page 60: *Hope Clark: <hope@fundsforwriters.com.*

Page 62: "74 Poetry Contests that Pay," *Ardor Online Literary Magazine.* ardorlitmag.com.

Page 72: *American Songwriter.*

Page 73: *Gemtracks.*

Chapter 7

Page 74: *Wikimedia Commons*

Various Sources Consulted.

Chapter 8

Page 99: *Wikimedia Commons*

Page 100: OnlineBookClub.org

Page 104: Adam Enfroy, "27+ Best Web Hosting Services of 2021, May 21, 2021." <adamenfroy.com/best-web-hosting-services#.

Various Sources Consulted.

Chapter 9

None.

BIOGRAPHY OF ROY E. PETERSON
LTC, U.S. Army, Military Intelligence Retired

Photo: Captain Roy E. Peterson. Can Tho Vietnam, 1972.

LTC Roy Peterson served as an Assistant Army Attaché in Moscow during the peak of the Cold War Years from 1983- 1985, as the first U.S. Foreign Commercial Officer in the Russian Far East for the U.S. Department of Commerce with dual duty as a Visa Issuing Officer for the U.S. Department of State, and as the first IBM Regional Manager, Vladivostok, Russian Far East (1993-1995).

He was Commander, Portal Monitoring, On-Site Inspection Agency in Votkinsk, Russia and Commander of the 5th Military Intelligence Company, 18th Military Intelligence Battalion, 66th Military Intelligence Group.

LTC Peterson was trained in Russian, German, and Vietnamese and used all three languages in their respective theaters of operation.

LTC Peterson is a recognized international trade and Russian political/military consultant. Roy was a recent faculty member with the University of Phoenix teaching global business, marketing, sales, management, military intelligence, unconventional warfare, and international trade.

Roy Peterson is a poet, songwriter, and award-winning bass voice singer.

Writing Credentials

LTC Peterson has published more than 80 books, over 20 extensive secret intelligence studies, over 100 intelligence reports (unavailable), 2 MA theses, and 2 Institute publications. Throughout life he has written monographs, business proposals, and engaged in marketing, for which he has international credentials. He has written over 100 country, rock and gospel songs.

Military Intelligence Credentials

Analyst, National Security Agency
Phoenix Advisor MR IV Corps, The Delta, Vietnam.
Analyst, Defense Intelligence Agency.
Commander, Military Intelligence Company, Germany. Manager, Army Security Clearances.
1st Army Staff Intelligence Advisor, Pentagon.
Selected to replace Ollie North on Security Council. Presidential Rep. to Russia, On-Site Inspection Agency.
Army Attaché, Moscow.
Executive Officer, Intelligence Collection Unit
Honor Graduate, US Army Russian Institute.
Russian language fluency.
Human Intelligence Coordinator, 1st Gulf War.
Awarded Legion of Merit, Bronze Star.

Academic Credentials

BA, Hardin-Simmons, MA University of Arizona.
MA University of Southern California.
MBA University of Phoenix.
Ph.D., passed written and oral exams and remains ABD.
Defense Language Institute, Russian.
Graduate, U.S. Army Command and General Staff College.
Faculty Member, University of Phoenix.
Faculty Member, University of Maryland.
Faculty Member, University of Arizona.

Faculty Member, Western New Mexico University.
Faculty Member, Travel University International.
Graduate Assistant, American Government, Texas Tech.

Business Credentials

President, HPO International and TriCrown International.
VP, International Trade Company,.
VP, Investment Company.
VP and COO, Construction Development Company,.
VP Management Company.
Sold trucks to Russia.
1st USDOC Foreign Commercial Officer in Russian Far East. 1st IBM
Manager in Russian Far East.
Taught International Trade and Global Business Management.
Director New Business Development for ENSCO.
Wrote operational and technical proposal for EG&G on
        Strategic Arms Limitation Talks Contract.
President Export Company.

BOOKS AND PUBLICATIONS AUTHORED
ROY E. PETERSON (81)

Poetry Books (Also See Political Poetry)

A Child's Home Companion: Poems Children Love
All American New Holiday Classic Poems: 100 + Poems for Christmas...
Alien Inspired Verse: Poetry from the Universe
Alpen Splendor, Mountain Grandeur
Always Means Forever: Poetry So Clever Until the Twelfth of Never
America Needs Adult Advice
American Country Poetry: From the Prairie to the Parlor
American Classic Poetry: Poetry for the Majority
American Gold Classic Poetry: If it doesn't Rhyme
American Heartland: Poetry, Wit, and Wisdom
American Heritage Poetry Collection
American Patriot Salute
Angels All Around Us: A Great Garden of Verse
A Pink Moon in April: Poetry from the Periphery
As the World Burns: Poetry by the Fireside
Autumn Echoes: Poetic Treasure Trove...
Beauty Begets Emotion: Rhymes of Love and Devotion
Before I Go to Bed: Poetry for Dreaming
Between Darkness and Light
Beyond the Back Seat: Coming of Age Nostalgic Treat
Christian Poetry for the Heart and Soul
Classic Poetry Renaissance: Rhyme and Meter Make it Sweeter
Cultural Conservation Companion: Clever Poems for Smart Homes
Democratic Party Down the Rabbit Hole: Descent into Political Madness
Dreamers Dream While Poets Scheme: Poets Pursue the Theme
Eternal Spring: Poetry and Promise
Fables from the Funny Farm: Follies, Frolic, and Fun
Feet on the Ground: Heart in the Sky
For Love May Find You: Poetry with Passion
Grains of Sand: Poetry by the Sea
Guardian Angel: All My Tomorrows
Guide to Self-Publishing Poetry
Happy Haunting Halloween: Olde and New Classics
Harmony and Discord in an Atonal World: Revelations.....
Love is Made in Heaven/Romance is Made on Earth
Love That Lasts Eternally: Poetry of Romance and Mystery
McCamey Memories We All Share: Nostalgic Poems...
My Best Classic Poetry Collection: Arrows Sent in Your Direction

My Heart Has Not Forgotten: Where'er Thine Feet Have Trodden
Mystery Has an Accomplice: Poems You Won't Want to Miss
Out of the Shadows: My 110 Best Nature Poems
Poems for Happy Times Treasury: My Own Selected Best Classical Poetry
Poetry Knocking on the Door: Classic Rhymes
Poetry is Passion: Truth and Time in Classic Rhyme
Poetry When Nights are Stormy: Classic Poems to Warm the Heart
Race Relations Objective Perspective Poetry
Riveting Romantic Love Treasury: Vol 2 My Own Selected Best Classical Poetry
Songs from a Sultry Soul
Sonnets from the Inner Sanctum: Poetry for Posterity
Sonnets from the Mellow Breeze
Southern Comfort: New Classic Poetry from Me
Texas Stardust
Texas Trail Dust: Cowboy Campfire Collection
Treasury of Wit, Wisdom and Advice: Vol 3 My Own Selected Best Class. Poetry
What the Heart Proposes: The Poet Discloses
Whither My Love: Treasury of Great Classical Love Poetry
When I Think of Heaven: Inspirational Sonnets, Soliloquies, Songs…
Where Love Dares to Go: Pathways Only Poets Know
Where the Foxes Play: Poetry to Read When the Fur Flies
While the Wind is Whispering Through the Sylvan Glen
Winter Casts Its Spell: Autumn Says Farewell

Poems Published by Prestigious Society of Classical Poets (18)

July 4th Celebration, 2018 (July 4, 2018)
The Poet's Soul with Artful Pen (November 25, 2018)
The Sordid Socialists and Cultish Communists (November 25, 2018)
The Commie Will Hijack a Word (November 25, 2018)
Where the Heart Goes (April 13, 2019)
In the Silence of the Evening (April 13, 2019)
If I Could Paint a Portrait (April 13, 2019)
Solemn Legion of the Brave (May 27, 2019)
May Old Glory Always Wave (July 4, 2019)
Veterans Day (November 11, 2019)
Why I Value Toilet Paper (March 17, 2020)
Solemn Silent Soldiers Rest (May 22, 2020)
Hearts and Clouds (January 14, 2021)
Though Worlds May Die and Silent Be (February 14, 2021)
Lives There the Man (March 14, 2021)
Gun Control is Mind Control (April 10, 2021)
The Seven Dwarves of Old Age (April 18, 2021:)
Epitaphs (May 13, 2021)

Poems Published by Western Poetry
Writers of the Purple Sage (May 2013)
Tucson Sunday Morning (February 2014)
Poem Published by Hardin-Simmons University
"Night Storm." <u>Quiet Thoughts</u>. Hardin-Simmons University, 1963.

Special Accolades
Featured Writer, Society of Classical Poets. <u>Journal,</u> 2019.
Featured Writer, Society of Classical Poets. <u>Journal,</u> 2020.
Featured Writer, Western Writers, 2014.

History
American Attaché in the Moscow Maelstrom
Fight of the Phoenix
Soviet Intelligence Process (Out of Print Monograph)
The Velvethammer: Lieutenant Colonels Get Things Done

Historical Fiction
From Chapultepec to Castle Gap
Hitler's Secret Jet Designer: Jet Invention, Austrian Connection…
Iron Ikon: U.S. Foreign Commercial Officer Duty in the Russian Far East
Russian Bears/American Affairs
Russian Romance: Danger and Daring

Humor, Wit and Wisdom
Peterson Perspective: Humor, Wit and Wisdom

Juvenile
Albert: The Cat That Thought He Could Fly

Life Stories (Memoirs)
On the Edge of Night: Finding Love Again at 70 (Vol II Horny Toads Trilogy)
Pansy, The Texas Trapeze Artist
Paths Upon the Prairie
When Sunsets Glow: Finding Lost Love in Life's Afterglow (Vol III Horny Toads)
Where the Horny Toads Play (Vol I Horny Toads Trilogy)

Politics
American Made Crisis: Aliens in Our Midst
Demolishing the Demons: Theology and Politics Preparing for the New Crusade
Gray Power Politics: Political Wants and Needs of the Newly Powerful Cross-cutting
      Demographic Segment

<u>**Relationships**</u>

Magnetism to Marriage
Men and Divorce

<u>**Major Business Proposals**</u>

INF Treaty Portal Monitoring Proposal
Victorville 442-Unit Apartment Complex

<u>**Three Masters Degree Theses**</u>

1. MA, Political Science, University of Arizona, 1969.
2. MA, International Relations, University of Southern California, 1970.
3. MBA, Global Business Management, University of Phoenix, 2001.